THE
AUTISM
PARTNER
HANDBOOK

How to Love an Autistic Person

Joe Biel, Elly Blue, and Dr. Faith G. Harper, LPC-S, ACS, ACN

T0001563

Microcosm Publishing
Portland, Ore | Cleveland, Ohio

THE AUTISM PARTNER HANDBOOK
How to Love an Autistic Person

© 2023 Joe Biel, Elly Blue, and Faith G. Harper

© This edition Microcosm Publishing 2023
First edition - 3,000 copies - April 11, 2023
ISBN 9781648411724
This is Microcosm #573
Cover and Design by Joe Biel
Illustration on page 43 by Eliot K Daughtry
Edited by Olivia Rollins

To join the ranks of high-class stores that feature Microcosm titles, talk to your local rep: In the U.S. **COMO** (Atlantic), **ABRAHAM** (Midwest), **BOB BARNETT** (Texas, Oklahoma, Louisiana), **IMPRINT** (Pacific), **TURNAROUND** (Europe), **UTP/MANDA** (Canada), **NEW SOUTH** (Australia/New Zealand), **GPS** in Asia, Africa, India, South America, and other countries, or **FAIRE** in the gift market.

For a catalog, write or visit:
Microcosm Publishing
2752 N Williams Ave.
Portland, OR 97227
https://microcosm.pub/Autism

Did you know that you can buy our books directly from us at sliding scale rates? Support a small, independent publisher and pay less than Amazon's price at **www.Microcosm.Pub**

Library of Congress Cataloging-in-Publication Data

Names: Biel, Joe, author. | Harper, Faith G., author.
Title: The autism partner handbook : how to love someone with autism / Joe Biel & Faith G. Harper, PhD.
Description: Portland : Microcosm Publishing, [2023] | Summary: ""Learn key communication skills for succeeding in a neurologically mixed relationship, gain a better understanding of your autistic partner's mental processes, troubleshoot your sex life, and level up your appreciation for their relationship strengths. Autistic-allistic relationships can flourish, but there are a few consistent and predictable areas where they can get in trouble, which you can work through together once you know how to spot them""-- Provided by publisher.
Identifiers: LCCN 2022059582 | ISBN 9781648411724 (trade paperback)
Subjects: LCSH: Autism. | Autistic people--Social life and customs. | Autistic people--Family relationships.
Classification: LCC RC553.A88 B5198 2023 | DDC 616.85/882--dc23/eng/20230214
LC record available at https://lccn.loc.gov/2022059582"

MICROCOSM · PUBLISHING

MICROCOSM PUBLISHING is Portland's most diversified publishing house and distributor with a focus on the colorful, authentic, and empowering. Our books and zines have put your power in your hands since 1996, equipping readers to make positive changes in their lives and in the world around them. Microcosm emphasizes skill-building, showing hidden histories, and fostering creativity through challenging conventional publishing wisdom with books and bookettes about DIY skills, food, bicycling, gender, self-care, and social justice. What was once a distro and record label started by Joe Biel in a drafty bedroom was determined to be *Publishers Weekly*'s fastest-growing publisher of 2022 and has become among the oldest independent publishing houses in Portland, OR, and Cleveland, OH. We are a politically moderate, centrist publisher in a world that has inched to the right for the past 80 years.

Global labor conditions are bad, and our roots in industrial Cleveland in the '70s and '80s made us appreciate the need to treat workers right. Therefore, our books are MADE IN THE USA.

CONTENTS

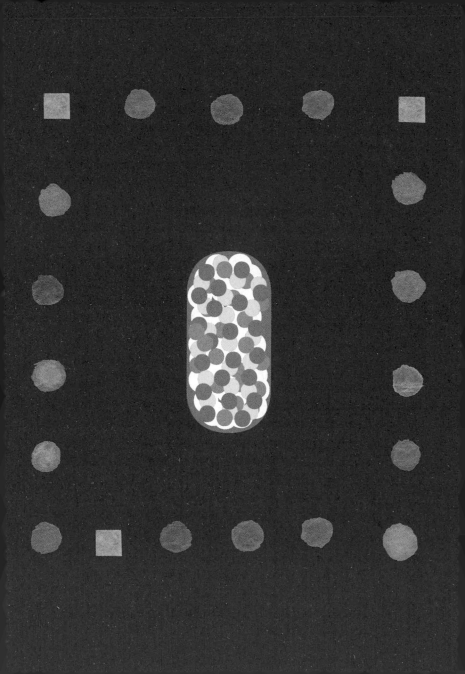

INTRODUCTION:
WHY THIS BOOK IS NEEDED

Love is more than a feeling or a thought: it's a behavior. Being in a relationship means being on the same *team*. That is, seeing and caring for each other's needs and facing the world together.

However, the needs of autistic people are often different from those of allistic people (people who lack the neurology and benefits of autism). This doesn't mean the two are fundamentally incompatible; every relationship requires time, effort, and listening to understand, instead of listening to respond. But it can present unique challenges. Allistic people often internalize the behavior of autistic people and interpret it as manipulative or critical, or as passive and infantile, rather than understanding it as expressing the autistic person's needs.

Hence this book. We wrote it for the allistic partners of autistic people who are trying to better understand their partners' worldview after growing up in a world that never taught them how to do so. Maybe your partner was diagnosed as autistic as a child, maybe as an adult. Maybe they just suspect that they are autistic. Maybe they don't know whether or not they are autistic—and aren't interested in finding out—but are clearly struggling, and you have strong suspicions. While diagnosis is a powerful tool for working towards a healthy self-image and a rewarding life, you also have power in how you manage being an ally and bridging the gap between your partner and the world. You don't have to talk about autism to talk about the ways that your partner interacts with society.

Autists are often perceived as strange or ridiculous, but allistic misunderstanding is a major part of the equation. This extends to all sorts of relationships, even business ones. For example, many years ago, my (Joe's) neurodivergent assistant would distribute the mail to all of the tenants in our building. Each day, he politely asked one particular person where to put their mail. This person didn't understand my assistant's social manner, decided that it was a passive-aggressive gesture, and refused to tell him where to put the mail. Somehow this culminated in me coming to work one day to find the tenant shouting that they should go fight in the parking lot and my assistant protecting his face.

This is just one example of how allistics often pathologize autistic people for their neurology. They don't understand autistic people and therefore read things into their behaviors that aren't there. And in romantic relationships, the stakes are especially high. But allistics can create strategies to help them better understand the needs of their neurodivergent partners and better communicate their own needs back. So while relationship issues will always arise, romantic or otherwise, the guidance in this book can help you to close these common gaps in understanding.

Most allistic people who are attracted to autistic people are caring, empathic nurturers who see and appreciate what makes autistic people complex and interesting. As a result, these neurologically mixed relationships tend to follow predictable and consistent patterns. Maxine Aston, a counselor for mixed couples and author of *Aspergers in Love*, describes a period of loving courtship, followed by a period in which the autistic partner becomes detached and bored or merely comfortable in the relationship. The allistic partner may feel like they've lost an empathic connection. They may attempt to salvage the relationship because they feel lonely or perhaps believe that they did something wrong. And the allistic partner's hurt becomes the responsibility of the autistic partner, which takes a severe toll on both of them. I (Joe) have found these patterns to be consistent in my own life and those of my autistic friends. But that doesn't mean that your relationship will perpetuate them, setting you up for failure. We're going to look at why these patterns are so pervasive and how to prevent them in your relationship.

We wrote this book because there was nothing like it. While there are many books about autism, few of them are by, for, or about autistic adults, and most don't acknowledge the complex, independent lives and relationships that many autistic people have built. And while there are a large number of books written by and for the parents of autistic children, we couldn't find any books written for the romantic partners of autistic people that acknowledged the autistic partner's perspective and needs as equally valid to those of the allistic partner. If all you know about autism is the infantilizing or coldhearted picture you find in most of the books that already exist, or in media like *Autism in Love*, it might be hard to imagine autistic people ever having an adult relationship in which they and their partner are equals, much less with an allistic person. But given that a presumed 1.59% of the population is autistic,[1] we have to imagine that these relationships are in fact pretty common. And in any relationship, sometimes you need support. That's where this book comes in.

WHO THIS BOOK IS FOR

Our assumption throughout this book is that the reader is an allistic person in an interabled romantic relationship with an autistic person, but we know that may not be you. If your partner, spouse, lover, or date is autistic (or signs point in that direction), this book is for you, regardless of your own neurology. And if you're the autistic partner of a neurotypical person, this book can help give you perspective on how you deserve to be treated and help you start

---

1 You may see other numbers. That's common. This statistic is based on the CDC's data reporting in 2020.

needed conversations in your relationship. You might also check out Faith and Joe's book *The Autism Relationships Handbook*, which is primarily for you, the autistic person, and *The Autism FAQ* (also by Faith and Joe), which is full of science-y shit that may help you better explain how your brain works to your one-in-particular.

You may also find this book helpful if you have an autistic person in your life in another capacity—child, family member, coworker, friend, etc. Or if your person isn't autistic, but has another form of neurodivergence, like attention-deficit/hyperactivity disorder (ADHD) or obsessive-compulsive disorder (OCD). At the same time, be aware that if you've met one autistic person, you've met exactly one autistic person—which is our polite way of saying that not everything in this book will apply to your partner, relationship dynamic, or scenario. And while we speak a lot about autism specifically, most of the guidelines in this book can help improve or clarify *any* relationship that suffers from misunderstandings, conflict, and loneliness. Faith can tell you that most of the principles here also apply in all the relationship counseling she does in her practice, and you honestly can't go wrong by listening, communicating straightforwardly, taking information at face value, and respecting and accommodating each other's different needs, rather than taking them personally.

Regardless of your relationship situation, the biggest messages you'll find here are as follows: Listen to your partner instead of assuming, work together to build a life that works for you both, and don't put yourself in the role of either a parent or a bully. When you get into an upsetting interaction, take a step back, count to three, and try to look at your situation in greater depth. (But the editorial team has decided that two sentences do not make a book, so we're going to go into more detail about what all of this looks like in day-to-day life.)

HOW TO USE THIS BOOK

We're going to begin by offering some general information about autistic people and relationships to establish a framework for understanding your interactions with your partner. You may think you have a firm grasp on relationships, but we're going to reframe many topics because of the way autistic brains work. We are going to assume that you are an allistic partner to an autistic person, but (as noted above) the advice in this book also applies to just about anyone in any relationship.

The first part of this book is about understanding the experiences and roles of each person in the relationship: your autistic partner and your own allistic self. We hope to strip away some of the myths and assumptions that many people carry into these relationships so that you can get past them in order to see your partner and yourself as you actually are and work on your relationship as such.

The second part of the book is focused on steps you can take to strengthen your relationship. How can you get along better? How can you improve your communication? How do you handle and repair conflicts? What about the logistics of daily life together, from major life decisions to giving each other gifts to dividing the housework? What about when you are together in social situations, walking down the street, or dealing with discrimination?

This book is based on both expertise and lived experience, which tends to be the most helpful combination. We want this to be easy to read and absorb, so we decided not to litter the text with a ton of footnotes or citations, but you can find a list of sources at the end, as well as a list of other books and resources we recommend.

WHO WE ARE

There are three of us writing this book: an autistic person, that person's allistic partner, and a therapist (who is not *their* therapist—but boy, would that be the recipe for a sitcom!).

Joe Biel (autigender/name only) ran away from a violent home as a teenager, 15 years before being diagnosed as autistic. After winding up at a punk rock club several nights per week during a formative life stage, then extending those punk concepts to the world of book publishing in 1996, Joe developed an artistic sensibility and value system based on these experiences. Having seen no healthy or successful models of relationships, Joe used to assume that all relationships were dysfunctional and wrought with conflict; however, Joe eventually participated in years of intensive therapy, which finally led to an autism diagnosis at the age of 32. The resulting series of events began opening doors instead of closing them and ultimately led to a period of stability that continues in the present. It's amazing that when you don't anticipate conflict in every interaction and—more importantly—you know how to resolve any actual conflict that (inevitably) arises, life progresses rather smoothly.

Elly Blue (she/her) has been the editor of many other books written by both Joe and Faith, but she is stepping into a coauthor role for this one, since she and Joe are partners and we figured she could be a relatable voice for her fellow allistic people with autistic partners. She came into the relationship somewhat feral and had a lot to learn in order to be a contributing member of a functional partnership based on trust and mutual respect. The biggest thing she's learned is to really listen to what other people say and take their words at face value—and also to really hear what she herself is saying, which is often not at all what she literally means. These skills have led to her becoming a much better partner in particular and communicator in general. Thanks, Joe!

Joe and Elly's relationship is basically another character in this book. They have been life partners since 2009 and business partners since 2015. Joe was diagnosed with autism about a year after they began dating, and their growing understanding of what that meant became tied up in their own individual growth and the cementing of their relationship, with plenty of humorous misunderstandings along the way.

Faith (she/im) is just another therapist. And not even a neurodivergent one. She is, however, from a family with strong neurodiversity game, because apparently all families should have one boring "normie" in their midst. To their further horror, she's also cis and straight, hence her overachieving herself into a doctorate. Freakin' weirdo. But being a therapist with lived experience as an allistic in the land of neurodiversity has served her well. She definitely didn't learn shit about neurodiversity in graduate school, but after accidentally becoming the therapist for both autists and their confused and exhausted but still loving partners, she has continued to seek out training on these topics, read everything she can get her hands on, and listen to what her neurodivergent clients are telling her about their lives. She also has completed a postdoc in sexology. Yes, this is a thing that exists, and yes, this makes her a sexologist. So the pragmatic aspects of relationship work are totally her jam, as long as you can forgive her for being allistic. She's written a lot of books and taught a lot of courses and workshops related to mental health for both individuals and couples. She likes the science-y part an awful lot and will drop in a lot of the details as we go through this book.

PART ONE:
UNDERSTANDING AUTISM

*T*his first part of the book has two chapters. The first is aimed at helping you better understand aspects of your partner's experience as an autistic person. It's so easy in any relationship, especially a long-standing one, to rely on old narratives or assumptions about each other. Every autistic person is different. Your partner might be a picky eater who thrives on going to noisy dance parties with flashing lights where they can stim by dancing enthusiastically. They may have trouble focusing on their goals, or they may have developed an elaborate system of checklists to help them be very successful in their chosen pursuit. They are likely brave enough to reframe a problem when you come to them complaining—whether you appreciate this or not. They might struggle to hold on to gainful employment, or they might be the CEO of the growing multimillion-dollar company they started while simultaneously having difficulty taking care of themselves. They might struggle socially in some situations *and* have a wide network of close friendships. They may not always understand the impact of their actions, but they may have new perspectives on yours. We hope this part of the book serves as a framework for observing, asking questions, and talking about your partner's experiences and needs; perhaps it has never occurred to either of you that these needs could, in fact, be accommodated.

The second chapter is about you, the autistic person's partner, particularly if you are not autistic. It's aimed at showing you some of the privileges you might take for granted, the common pitfalls that allistic partners encounter in interabled relationships, and the strengths you can bring to the relationship to create a healthier, more equitable, lasting bond between you and your partner.

A NOTE ABOUT LANGUAGE

There are a lot of different ways to talk about autism, and you'll find that not all autistic people have the same perspective on how we are perceived, how we are talked about, or how we want to be treated. Largely this is because of how power works in society. Just as the victors are the ones who get to write the historical narrative of the war that was waged, it is the majority (allistics) that shapes autistic stories and defines "the rules" that we all "have" to follow. As a result, many autistic people internalize the views of allistics and begin to see themselves as lesser and incapable. Yet many autistic people are over it and don't like being depicted through other people's framing and ideas about what is "normal."

In this book, we don't say Asperger's. This is for two reasons: (1) the term Asperger's stems from U.S. and Nazi eugenics, a popular movement in the 1930s U.S. that advocated "cleansing" the gene pool of defects and was repeatedly cited by Hitler as the inspiration for World War Two;[2] and (2) science simply has a better understanding of the brain today and accepted in 2013 that autism and Asperger's were actually the same. When "Asperger's syndrome" was removed from the APA's fifth edition of the *Diagnostic and Statistical Manual of Mental Disorders* (*DSM-5*) in 2013, many autistic people balked. Asperger's was how they thought of themselves—an important part of their identity. For this reason, some people hold on to this label, and that's their choice. But for most, it will slowly disappear. We are just "autistic people" now.

---

2 Hans Asperger worked in Nazi eugenics programs based on the ideas of U.S. eugenicist Madison Grant. Herr Hans was a public proponent of racial hygiene, which is an in-polite-company term for forced sterilization and even "euthanasia" of children. He was a total piece of shit. The attempts to shed that history have been awkward and clumsy, but worst of all, these eugenic ideas delayed autistic diagnosis in the U.S. for decades because of the idea that anyone with the diagnosis was lesser. For more on this, check out *Asperger's Children: The Origins of Autism in Nazi Vienna* by Edith Sheffer.

We say "autistic person" instead of "person with autism." This is because autism is not something that you could ever fundamentally separate from the person. Autism is not an enclosure with an allistic person inside of it. In one cartoon by the Autistic Avenger, the left panel depicts a person carrying luggage with the caption "person with autism." The right panel depicts a person with the luggage inside their head and the caption "autistic person." The trouble is that well-meaning people have spent years training themselves to use the "person-first" language popularized by the second wave of the disability rights movement. Person-first language means not defining someone by their traits, behaviors, or descriptor. You might say "person driving a car" instead of "driver" or "person who frequently makes exasperated and excited comments" instead of "shouter." In some cases, this is desirable, as when people don't want to be defined by a temporary or externally imposed condition, like homelessness or a broken leg, or by, say, the divorce rates of people who commute by car. However, autism is different. The autistic community has repeatedly declared that our personhood is *not* separate or removable from our autism. Similarly, we say "is autistic" or "has been diagnosed with autism" instead of "has autism."

In this book, we don't talk much about autism as a disability, but rather as a neurological difference. We believe that autism is not inherently a flaw, and autistic people are not broken or wrong. But we do see that many expectations, assumptions, and sensory experiences in the modern world make autism a disabling condition, and people claiming autism as a disability are not wrong to do so. Disability is relative: if we did not have the technology to create vision-correcting lenses, most people who wear glasses or contacts today would be disabled by their vision limitations. We're envisioning a world where it's acceptable or even encouraged to stim in public and speak with blunt directness, where technology and architectural standards are designed to limit overwhelming sounds, smells, and crowds, and where autistic people are given equal respect, rights, safety, and accommodation. It doesn't have to be a disability.

More on this later, but we don't use language like "high functioning" and "low functioning," as an individual's level of function isn't fixed but rather varies based on the circumstances. And by the same token, we no longer talk about autism as being on a spectrum. Different people might have different support needs, coping skills, co-occurring conditions, or trauma histories, but you're either autistic or you aren't.

Even so, use the language desired by the person to whom you are referring. Don't out someone who doesn't feel safe to be outed. When in doubt, it's always best to respect the wishes of the person you're talking with about what language they want to be used for them in any specific context. This may be different in different situations—e.g., your partner may prefer to be referred to by their birth-assigned name and pronouns and not have autism discussed in front of their grandparents but be more open within your friend group. Most interactions are influenced by context. Life is the real spectrum, isn't it? And that's okay.

CHAPTER 1: UNDERSTANDING YOUR AUTISTIC PARTNER

*A*utism is a pervasive state of neurology that affects all aspects of our personality, emotions, and experiences. As we've already stated, you cannot separate the person from their autism.

Autism is also widely misunderstood. Being autistic involves hundreds of encounters where "friends" and strangers alike tell you, "You don't seem like you have autism" or "Are you *sure* that you have autism?" If you respond by asking a few journalistic questions like "What do you mean?" or "Can you explain?" they often realize that they don't know what autism is or how it functions. More importantly, they cannot fathom what autistic life is like.

To understand autistic people's experiences today, you need to know a little history. The word "autism," which has been in use for about 100 years, comes from the Greek word "autos," meaning "self." The term describes conditions in which a person is removed from social interaction, thereby functioning as an isolated self. Eugen Bleuler, a Swiss psychiatrist, was the first person to use the term, around 1911. He referred to autism as one group of symptoms of schizophrenia.[3] We no longer think of autism as childhood-onset schizophrenia or even related to it.

In the 1940s, researchers in the U.S. began to use the term "autism" to describe children with emotional or social problems.

---

3 Even through the 1960s, treatment professionals continued to view autism as a form of schizophrenia, meaning they believed that autism was a thought disorder that causes someone to see, hear, smell, or feel things that others do not and to believe things that are empirically false. Autism is not a thought disorder and autistic people don't tend to be delusional, even though echoes of this misconception live on in popular culture.

Leo Kanner, a doctor at Johns Hopkins University, used it to describe the withdrawn behavior of several children he studied. At about the same time, Hans Asperger, an Austrian psychiatrist, identified a similar condition, eventually called Asperger's syndrome (though, as we've discussed, we no longer use this term). Once there was a realization that autism was a different form of neurodivergence and did not include symptoms of a thought disorder like schizophrenia, treatments focused on punishment-based curative strategies, like electroshock therapy and LSD, to attempt to change autistic brains. Ideas rooted in eugenics were so prevalent in the U.S. that the condition was largely swept under the rug, not thought about or accepted. It wasn't until the 1980s that treatment professionals started looking at behavioral strategies and adaptations to learning environments to help autistic people live the best lives possible in a neuronormative world.

This historical background is important to understanding why there is still so little study or science regarding autism. These problems go back hundreds of years and remain unresolved. One result of a lack of study is a lack of appropriate care. Thus autistic people often suffer from intergenerational trauma. "Intergenerational trauma" is another term for epigenetic trauma, which means that the things that happen to you affect how your genes express, and those gene expressions get passed down to future generations. Through this process, a person's descendents can inherit the fear, trepidation, and response instincts needed to live in an unsafe world. Autism is frequently an inherited condition that comes packaged with an inherited trauma response because of how our ancestors were treated, largely due to being undiagnosed and misunderstood. (For more information about trauma, see the section devoted to it later in this chapter.)

The increased prominence and understanding of autism over the past 10 years has come along with a lot of misconceptions. It's really only in the past 30 years that autism has been widely recognized in the U.S., which is important to understanding why it feels like it's "suddenly everywhere." So we'll just say it right here: Autism is not curable. It's not caused by vaccines. Autism cannot be traced back to any singular origin. Those of us newly struggling with a diagnosis want answers, and if there was a simple answer with a simple solution, we'd have a good inkling by now. However, life is messy and the etiology of autism is just as messy as the vast majority of diagnoses we use to label individuals.

WHAT IT'S LIKE TO BE AUTISTIC

Autism is best understood by learning what it is like to be autistic. Joe has found that generally autism involves variations on eight things:

- We have about 42% more resting brain activity than most people. Our senses and our brains notice more stuff. Sometimes that's light or heat or visual detail or flavor. Some theorists refer to this as "sensory issues." Others use the phrase "Intense World Theory." Regardless of what you call it, this increased resting brain activity is why autistics throughout history have filled such vital roles as inventors, composers, problem solvers, and developers. We are good at noticing stuff and imagining a different approach to it.[4]

- We get exhausted because of all of this information. This results in stress symptoms, meltdowns, and the need for time alone.

---

4 This might be why I am so successful as a book publisher, running the fastest-growing independent publishing company in 2022 according to *Publishers Weekly*.

- 98.41% of other people are a cryptic, irrational mess that makes no sense. Which is to say that they are "not autistic." Doctors call this aspect of autism "difficulty socializing."

- We operate based on a series of complex and elaborate rules that get more complicated every day. Life is like a to-do list and we check a lot of boxes. Other people keep changing the interpretation of the rules and adding more boxes to check, so it feels like they're messing with us all the time.

- It's hard to understand what other people are thinking or feeling unless they tell us in plain, exact language or we have a lot of history together. For some reason, most people are very uninclined to state their thoughts and feelings plainly, or even *say what they mean*. Other people sometimes feel like we are messing with them. This is confusing and alienating for both neurologies, and it makes it difficult to build shared history. Doctors call this difficulty understanding others a deficit in our "theory of mind."

- Stimming, or self-stimulatory behavior, is present in almost all autistic people, according to researchers. Stimming takes many, many forms. Some people find ways of doing it subtly, like drumming with their fingers, so as to not make others uncomfortable; but regardless, we're doing it. Most of us open and close our hands repeatedly or make repetitive motions like flapping our appendages. Stimming helps us to relax and be present in our bodies.

- We are fixated on cool stuff. When I was five I liked dolls and action figures. Then I loved Legos deeply. For a year I glued together models of dinosaurs and recited every fact about them. Soon I abandoned that for Dungeons & Dragons, but that was a little too social for me, so I found punk rock and memorized all of the facts about that. Then, 27 years ago, I became a publisher, and I have been able to turn that into a new, exciting adventure every day. I often realize that I've been talking about a subject for way too long to someone who is politely disinterested and doesn't know how to kill the conversation. Doctors call this "persistent, intense preoccupations."

- It's hard for autistic people to break goals down into actionable steps and see their actions the way allistics do. Doctors call this skill "executive function" and find that autistics have trouble connecting the dots. I know a number of autistics who have multiple master's degrees but have never had a job and don't know how to get one. It's as if someone wanting to be a successful clinical therapist just kept sweeping this one part of the floor and organizing their desk and waiting for clients to come to them. Similarly, people apply for jobs for money and power, but it can be difficult to understand that you have to lie and say "challenges and opportunities" instead.

While some of these symptoms might be more or less pronounced than others—or it may not be immediately apparent that a symptom is being experienced, especially if the person has not been diagnosed or does not know they are autistic—we experience the vast majority of them every day in a way that fundamentally changes the nature of our lived experience.

DIAGNOSIS

Yes, you will see pearl-clutching articles every few years about the rates of autism going up, so let's talk about what that really means. The increase in the number of people receiving the diagnosis has gone up not because the rates of autism are increasing at warp speed, but because we are getting better at recognizing autism for what it is. Was it a new vaccine on the market? Nope, we just got an updated diagnostic manual that better defined autism.[5]

Diagnosis is a powerful tool that can validate someone's experience by giving it a name. It can point the way towards other tools and knowledge that can make life a whole lot easier. It can open up the door to accessing support and accommodations. It can give the people in the autist's life a lens through which to understand and appreciate them, rather than taking their differences and struggles personally. But it can have downsides as well—for instance, some people have jobs in which a formal diagnosis could be a threat to their security clearance or employment. You can read quite a bit more about obtaining a diagnosis in *The Autism FAQ*.

For almost everyone I (Joe) knew who was diagnosed properly, the diagnosis remains the greatest epiphany in their lives—the moment that adult life began. It's an explanation that helps to make sense of a very confusing and painful past, putting it into a coherent context where it no longer feels like a horrible web of pain but instead becomes a clear road map to future decision making and behavior. After diagnosis, taking fault for our behavior becomes much easier for autistics. We gradually trust others, see their motives, and no longer feel under attack all the time. We start to see everyone's behavior and decisions in context rather than in black and white, and we are often embarrassed to look back at our lives and see how we reacted in the past.

---

5 The *DSM-5* also defines autism's new sister diagnosis, social communication disorder (SCD), which was added to describe people who consistently struggle with social skills and communication skills but do not demonstrate the restrictive/repetitive behavior criteria required for a diagnosis of autism spectrum disorder (ASD).

I found a diagnostic professional who understood and recognized symptoms in adults and charged only a few hundred dollars. For me, it truly felt like life began at diagnosis. Every painful mistake suddenly made sense and I felt like I finally had a blueprint for leading a happy, healthy, and successful life. And since I had gone through the trouble of getting a proper diagnosis at 32 years old, it used to annoy me when I met self-diagnosed autistic people. But in hindsight, I can see that I got very lucky. Due to a variety of obstacles, very few autistic adults get definitive diagnoses. Autistics over 35 are often diagnosed when our children are, but many slip through the cracks.

Part of this is related to how we transmute our internal experience into something more socially appropriate. As autistics move into adulthood, we become better and better at masking our symptoms. We often mimic other people's performances that are well-received. This is why you might see autistic people performing characters or lines from a movie or TV show or retelling a popular person's jokes. But rest assured, their autistic symptoms will always eventually appear. Our imitation of an allistic person cannot last forever, and the daily challenges become apparent even in the best actors. Give us support, space, and encouragement that it's okay to pursue our special interests even if it means that we'll spend less time with you.

Additionally, life before diagnosis is very confusing, and we suffer a lot of trauma without understanding what is an acceptable way for others to treat us. This almost always results in heightened anxiety and depression, which in turn begin to obscure our symptoms of autism, further confusing the people around us. Autistic people are at vastly higher risk of depression, anxiety, and suicide than the general population. Conditions such as these, as well as trauma and bipolar disorder, make it difficult for a diagnostic clinician to see the symptoms of autism; the cloud of co-occurring symptoms tends to trick diagnostic criteria.

Add to these issues a lack of access to adequate healthcare and lack of training for healthcare professionals, and you have a real toxic sludge of a problem. Proper testing can also cost thousands of dollars or be denied for bureaucratic and liability reasons,[6] which only serves to divide people and prevent them from knowing the truth. And the issue can be further compounded by factors like gender and race. While you will see statistics that "demonstrate" that autism occurs far more frequently in individuals assigned male at birth and socialized as males, the actual difference in autism rates by sex is likely statistically insignificant. The criteria for diagnosing autism are based on how it presents in boys, and it's also much harder for women and girls to get a diagnosis because they are pressured to master social skills and emotional labor from a young age, which leads to increased masking of their symptoms. Similarly, while transgender people are far more likely than cisgender people to qualify for an autism diagnosis, they must weigh other considerations when seeking diagnosis, such as discrimination or the possibility that an autism diagnosis could be used to invalidate their transness. People of color also get better at masking their autism because of pressure to behave in ways that make society (read: dominant, white culture) more comfortable. Essentially, the further someone is from the top of the power structure, the more difficult it becomes for them to get a definitive stamp of "autistic" once they are an adult.

---

6 Due to the eugenic history of autism, many specialists are hesitant to diagnose autism because they still perceive an autism diagnosis as imposing limitations on the patient. In many ways, autistics are seen as lesser, and since diagnoses are given based on symptoms and behaviors (rather than, for example, blood tests), doctors are worried about diagnosing too freely.

Diagnosis is a huge life milestone. The process itself can be difficult, expensive, and traumatic. And the immediate fallout isn't necessarily easy, though many people find it a relief in the short term and life changing for the much, much better in the long term. But like any huge life change or revelation, it can come with an adjustment period—a transformation of identity or priorities as the person settles into their new skin, realizing who they really are. There can be a lot of justified anger and sadness about the way they were treated and the compromises made before diagnosis. They'll likely be learning a lot and incorporating that information quickly. They may lash out because they don't yet know how they feel about any given conversation and everything starts to feel like an attack. These things settle over time as the new identity sets in.

Some of you are likely reading this book because your partner hasn't been diagnosed yet and you're trying to figure out what's up with them. In the next chapter, we have some advice about how to handle bringing up the topic of autism with your partner if this is not something you've discussed together yet. But there are ways of recognizing autism without diagnosis as well. Does this person have a unique gait? Do they have poor or peculiar posture? Do they move their arms while they walk like no one you've ever seen? Do they confuse left and right? Can they talk about a special interest for hours while you demonstrate disinterest and resistance with your body language? Do they perform repetitive behaviors or speak in a monotone? Do their rituals seem to have no point or outcome? Does humor seem difficult for them to grasp? Do they lack interest in activities that require coordination? Do they misjudge the distance between themselves and objects in their environment? Are they having a hard time recognizing or responding to your emotions— or their own? Do they have a unique vocabulary? Do they appear to be disorganized? Do they have a unique style, with clothes that seem to have worn out long ago? Do they seem ambivalent about the people around them while expressing intense compassion and empathy toward unlikely things, like a stray dog that they've never met? More than a few of these and you are probably dealing with an autistic person. (However, as we explain in the next chapter, it is never a good idea to diagnose your partner yourself; this list of traits is only meant to give you a general idea of what the signs are.)

AUTISM IN LOVE

So what does all this mean for romantic relationships? As the allistic partner, you may be worried that your autistic one-in-particular is incapable of a relationship. No flexibility or connection? Can't even have a conversation? What am I then, their nanny and housekeeper?

Contrary to popular belief and pop culture, being autistic doesn't mean someone is inherently going to have relationship difficulties. But the expectations of the people they date (and of the neurotypical world as a whole), combined with the way many autistic people are socialized, lead to some predictable relationship hurdles:

- Many autistic people weren't understood by their family of origin, meaning they are mostly self-raised and self-taught and may also have a considerable trauma history. This may be compounded by discrimination in many aspects of their lives. As a result, they may have ingrained habits that make sense to them but that might not make sense to another person and also might not be healthy.

- Many autistic people, especially those diagnosed young, may have been raised to see themselves as helpless and may need to learn later in life to pursue meaningful goals, develop independent life skills, and pull their own weight in an adult relationship.

- Many allistics bring expectations to their relationships based on cultural norms that may not make any sense, or even register at all, to their autistic partners.

- Many allistics see autistics as incapable, rather than simply *different* in their understanding of any given problem or situation.

Your autistic partner may be facing one, two, or, perhaps most likely, all of these hurdles. Overcoming the first two is their responsibility; the last two are yours. The good news is that they're all completely manageable.

But despite all this, autistic people's inherent neurology tends to be blamed for relationship failures.

Dr. Claire Jack, a therapist, autism advocate, and autistic person, has done a good job identifying the four core areas where most people assume autistic people experience failures and barriers in relationships. They are empathy issues, social issues, communication issues, and structure issues. While it's true that many autistic people do experience all four issues in relationships, so do allistic people. Our approaches to identifying and resolving such issues may be different depending on our neurology and other factors, but these are all very human. Let's do some mythbusting.

Empathy Issues: Despite their reputation for being cold and emotionless, autistic people have enormous wells of compassion and empathy and can feel with other people with astounding perception and depth. They struggle with what is termed "cognitive empathy," meaning one's ability to read another human being's experience in their voice, expressions, and behavior, because of their deficit in mirror neurons. Someone who is autistic may not "read" from your tight voice and expression that you are in pain, but once it has been communicated to them they have a profound ability and desire to understand, share, and support your experience of pain. Give them a chance. We have a lot more to say about this later in this chapter.

Social Issues: While autistic people may struggle with social cues and skills, this is not necessarily true in relationships where you spend so much time together that you really get to know one another's inner lives. The same struggle with mirror neurons applies here, too. Imagine being in a room of aliens with an entirely different language, set of behavioral norms, and cultural ideology. You're desperate for cues as to what is going on and how you are meant to interact. Eventually you get exhausted and overwhelmed and either shut down entirely or explode from frustration. That's the experience of an autistic person in a crowd that feels unsafe. It is not the case with one or two safe people with whom communication strategies, wants, and needs have been established. In fact, most autistic people will tell you they feel incredibly safe in these haven relationships, just like allistics. Once you and your partner have grown to know and trust each other, you'll likely find them far better company than anyone else.

Communication Issues: Communication is a struggle for most everyone, neurodivergent or not. Modern humans tend to code their conversations, right? "No worries" generally means *so many worries* (and you are likely in deep shit). An autistic person, who isn't fabulous at cognitive empathy, becomes overwhelmed and shuts down on communication.

But what happens when you communicate in a way that's concrete as pavement? What if, instead of saying "No worries," we say, "Today was awful for me, my boss yelled at me for something they did wrong and then I missed the bus and got stuck in the sleet. I am desperately in need of a mug of hot tea and a snuggle and a dumb movie with you, is that possible?" We offer a lot of perspective and advice on emotions and communication later in this book.

Structure Issues: Again, autistic people have a reputation for requiring rigid, unvarying routines. And this reputation is in some ways earned, but it doesn't hold true in every situation or for every person. Remember that statistic about having 42% more brain activity? That shit is exhausting, so maintaining a more soothing and consistent outside world helps an autist better manage their life. They will likely also hyperfixate on something that is important to them (remember how Joe memorized all those facts about dinosaurs and punk rock?). Can that be an issue in a relationship? Sure. Especially if you're the type of person who loves to go with the flow and see where life leads you. But that can also be a challenge if you have an allistic partner who's a big planner. My (Faith's) neurodivergent work hubby for years would tease me that planning a therapy group with me was like planning a vacation with his mother. But it was truly a tease; I'd organize the fuck out of everything and he would go with the flow. Since teamwork makes the dream work, honoring what each of you brings to the table and speaking to the preferences and needs of both parties can go a long way in preventing both dysregulation and resentment. We'll get into more strategies for working together in the second part of this book, pinky swear.

So, remember what we were saying at the beginning of this section about the allistic partner's expectations being a relationship hurdle? These are some examples of exactly the sort of expectations that can do more harm than good, no matter how good your intentions. Not everything you'll learn about autism, including in this book, will exactly apply to your relationship. Your autistic partner might struggle with all these issues in a textbook way, or they might be great at expressing and understanding emotions, a social butterfly, a skilled communicator, spontaneous and easygoing, or some/all of the above depending on the moment.

AUTISTIC ABILITIES

We're going to break down core aspects of autistic experience in this chapter, but we want to start by talking about the autistic superpowers that don't get enough recognition: the things that can make us amazing partners.

Autistic people have incredibly strong moral codes, loyalties, and trustworthiness. If you're clear and direct about what you want from your partner, they can give that to you. The autistic ability to pursue and solve problems can really take the pressure off of you once you embrace this habit. The flip side of this is that you must also prompt and listen to your partner talk about their needs and wants so that the relationship is mutual.

Let's look at some other things autistic partners can offer.

• *Autistic people have a surprising ability to perceive things.* Probably due to intellectually interfacing with others' emotions, autistic people possess something of a "sixth sense." For example, I (Joe) was once on the phone with someone.

She answered a call on the other line and disappeared for a few minutes. Through a process of educated deduction, I realized that it was her ex-boyfriend, calling her from a separate line in the same house because he was upset that I was on the phone with her. When she got back on the line, I explained all of this to her and she was stunned. "Yeah . . . but how did you know that?" She did not like the explanation that I was psychic.[7]

- *Autistic people see things from a different perspective.* Elly here—it may never have occurred to you the number of things that you don't *actually* have to do until your partner points out that those things are completely illogical and that you hate them. This includes big things like continuing in an unsatisfying career, planning to have children, or maintaining relationships that hurt you, as well as smaller things like eating food you dislike or wearing uncomfortable shoes. Joe often says things that seem far-fetched until I question my own assumptions—claiming, for instance, to be politically moderate when most people in today's U.S. would consider Joe's politics to be quite far to the left. But from a global perspective, Joe's views are actually pretty close to the center. This is just one example of how our autistic partners can help us look at ourselves and the world in unexpected ways.

- *Autistic people solve problems instinctively.* Scientists are still just beginning to study autism, but they're finding that autistic people are often inventors because their thinking is different. They recognize the problem and work backwards

7 Faith here. Before even visiting my house, Joe knew exactly which zines I owned and how I stored them. I got a text one day saying, "Hey, go get your box of sexual health zines, and send me *blah blah blah*." This was a logical deduction based on my behavior and personality; I guess I'm just that easy to clock. ;)

to the solution in a way that allistics don't. Through greater reaction to stimulus, autistic people notice more details. On my way into work one day, I (Joe) noticed that a piece of outdoor electrical conduit was sagging a centimeter lower than it normally does. Upon closer inspection it turned out to be full of water from a leaking downspout. As dangerous as this sounds, it's common for water to get into electrical conduit; but it needs to be dealt with. So I used two vice grips to loosen the unions and rotate the conduit so that the water could drain out through an existing hole. A dozen other people had walked past before me that morning and noticed nothing.

- *Autistic people want to make things better—all the time.* Autistic people have the magical ability to look at a system, see what's wrong with it, and find a way to fix it. This leads us to communicate honestly and bluntly, which is perhaps our most infamous trait. And this trait is often perceived differently based on the autistic person's gender. From autistic women especially, certain statements can come across as scathing criticism.[8] Thanks to the patriarchy, a woman saying the same thing as a man is going to be perceived as abrasive, rather than assertive. Meanwhile, in relationships and when facing emotionally loaded topics, autistic men are more inclined to withdraw than to confront—though they could give you an extended lecture on the best place to set up the projector and how to make your home stereo system sound better. Autistic men have almost always been repeatedly shamed into thinking they

---

8 In her book *Unfuck Your Friendships*, Faith wrote about a conversation where an autistic woman was asked by a friend if a dress made her look fat. And the woman, thinking it was a helpful and honest answer, said, "No, your fat makes you look fat." It wasn't a judgment at all, but was clearly perceived as one.

don't understand emotionally complex topics and have thus learned not to engage with them. Either way, the autistic dissatisfaction with and inability to tolerate people who are bad at their jobs is what makes us great at ours. It can be shocking and frustrating, but as long as you don't try to read into our behavior and find subtext or a game that isn't there, you will see what we mean. Isn't that refreshing? Perhaps that's why you're dating one of us.

- *Autistic people are great at developing a sense of humor.* Statistically, your autistic partner is very likely to be smarter than average. Not to shame the normies, but researcher Bernard Crespi refers to autism as a *disorder of high intelligence*, referring to several correlates of intelligence that autistic people tend to share, including brain activity, brain growth, deliberative decision making, attentional focus, and amazing visual-spatial abilities. Boo-ya, fancy! But most importantly for the continued growth of our relationships, we never lose our curiosity or desire to learn more. When I (Joe) wanted to learn how to do electrical wiring, I went to the library, sat down, and read the books. Similarly, I learned humor from mimicking comedies, doing the emotional labor of detangling what makes the jokes poignant or funny and then writing in a similar fashion. Humor should be a highly evolved form of critical thinking, revealing greater truths and only punching up, never down. It's a powerful tool for autistic people to connect all of the dots of their observations and work through complicated ideas in front of an audience that may not be ready for them. If your partner is into being funny, their jokes are probably going to be jaw-droppingly multi-layered and delivered in a total deadpan. But they may not be able to calibrate their humor perfectly to the audience and situation. If you're not sure, it's always totally okay to ask if they are joking or serious. If you think they're hilarious most of the time, it's a good sign for your relationship.

- *Autistic people are entrepreneurial.* Each time that I got a job, I would pick apart every flaw in the handling, systems, and material flow. This was appreciated if my intelligence was respected, but I quickly learned that most people aren't concerned with efficiency and would rather follow illogical orders. Autistic people can't do this. If a directive does not serve the stated goal, I find a method that makes more sense and pursue that instead. In the rare cases when I didn't get fired, I would eventually quit in disgust, shocked at how badly each company was being run. Eventually, I stumbled into my present self-employment scheme of 27 years: I founded and now manage a book publishing company with over 30 employees.

- *Autistic people look younger.* This is a bit of an outlier on this list, but in our youth-obsessed culture, looks are often perceived as an ability or advantage. We have less muscle tone in our faces, which results in our less expressive facial gestures. We usually look stoic. Autism is also associated with neoteny, the retention of juvenile traits, resulting in an even more youthful appearance. Additionally, it is easier for us to emotionally relate with children. Another understudied trait that may be neurologically related to neoteny is that every autistic person that I've ever met walks strangely—yet we each have a unique gait. I feel like that is the perfect metaphor for what you are signing up for: your autistic partner will share traits with other autistic people, but those traits will manifest in individual ways.

AUTISM AND TRAUMA

Trauma is not a symptom of autism, but we're talking about it here because your partner is very likely to have a lot of trauma. Trauma is often a product of how autistic people are treated by allistics and society at large, and it is so common among them that it clouds the ability of clinicians to diagnose adults. And there's nothing quite like unhealed trauma, whether it's on the part of an allistic partner or an autistic partner, to throw a wrench into an otherwise perfectly good relationship.

Trauma is an injury to the nervous system caused by events that we did not have the capacity or support to heal from. When you don't adequately process the trauma to understand what happened and why, the event becomes hard coded into your brain and affects your experience and behavior even after the danger has passed.

Why does the brain do this? Your brain's job, first and foremost, is to keep you alive. Your brain is hardwired to protect you, and in order to do so it's going to err on the side of caution. The brain uses shortcuts (psychologists call them "heuristics") to problem solve and make decisions quickly and without expending significant effort. Of course, this means it'll misfire and it won't always do a great job at assessing what is actually a threat and what isn't. So our brains' protective responses often end up doing the opposite—getting us into unhealthy patterns of behavior that hurt us and others.[9]

The brain performs essential survival tasks when something dangerous is going on, such as when early humans came face-to-face with a prehistoric house cat the size of a small sedan. The amygdala, the brain's fear processor, says, "I remember the last time this happened, it really hurt, which was bad!" And the brain stem

9 For so much more on trauma, the brain stem, and the brain science of trauma response, check out Faith's book *Unfuck Your Brain: Using Science to Get Over Anxiety, Depression, Anger, Freak-outs, and Triggers.*

tells the prefrontal cortex, "Let's get out of here so we don't get hurt again!" So we run away. Or we fight back. Or we freeze up and play dead and hope the situation passes us over.

Being able to assess threats and respond appropriately is a necessary survival skill and isn't problematic in and of itself. But when our threat system is activated continuously or in very extreme circumstances, it can end up staying turned on. A traumatic event is essentially anything that overwhelms our ability to cope, and if we don't achieve resolution and healing from these events, our brains continue to respond from this trauma-activated state. This can lead to these survival responses being frequently misapplied to situations where we feel under attack but aren't facing any real threat. All kinds of things can feel threatening.

Our experiences determine our expectations for the future, and thus form our reality. Our brains are fed a certain amount of raw data that is processed to draw conclusions about what is going on around us. They generalize and err on the side of safety. For example, if you have been attacked by a stranger in a dark alley, you may believe that this is a common event. If your previous employer went out of business suddenly without warning, you'd be concerned that your present employer will too, despite no evidence of this happening. If a friend abruptly ended a friendship in the past, it can feel like this is what friends do and you'll expect it in all future relationships because it's difficult to see how the circumstances are different now. It is through these same processes that, when you see a black-and-white photo of a banana, your brain interprets it to be yellow because of every banana that you've seen previously.

The classic way people talk about trauma is in reference to a horrific, singular event like a car crash or the loss of a loved one. But clinicians and the general public are starting to understand

Autism Spectrum Disorder   Post-Traumatic Stress Disorder

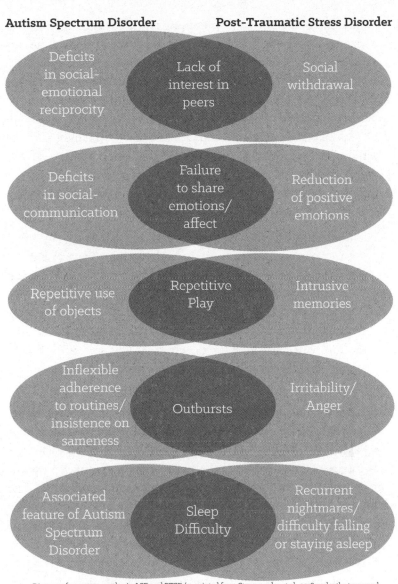

Deficits in social-emotional reciprocity | Lack of interest in peers | Social withdrawal

Deficits in social-communication | Failure to share emotions/affect | Reduction of positive emotions

Repetitive use of objects | Repetitive Play | Intrusive memories

Inflexible adherence to routines/insistence on sameness | Outbursts | Irritability/Anger

Associated feature of Autism Spectrum Disorder | Sleep Difficulty | Recurrent nightmares/difficulty falling or staying asleep

Diagram of symptom overlap in ASD and PTSD (re-printed from Stavropoulos et al., 2018 under the terms and conditions of the Creative Commons Attribution (CC BY) license (creativecommons.org/licenses/by/4.0/).

trauma more and more as also coming from a recurring, ongoing experience over time. What if every time you asked your parents a question, they yelled at you or ignored you? That might leave you with trauma. If you are told or shown over and over at any age that you aren't valued, aren't fully human, that's going to leave some hurts in need of repair. Do you get where we're going with this? A lot of what autistic people experience in both childhood and adulthood is traumatizing, and their brains are going to want to protect them from further harm by shutting down, lashing out, or using whatever other coping mechanisms they developed, probably as little kids, that may or may not serve them any longer.

I (Joe) was physically abused from a young age, so my brain expects to be treated this way throughout life. Consequently, I sometimes still put myself in situations where this could happen because it did not occur to me that I had other options when I was a child, and it's easy to regress to that thinking today. The combination of autism and trauma can often make it feel like choices are dictated for you and you have little or no control. This is exactly how a tripped threat-assessment system, when left unhealed, turns into a trauma response.

Faith here. Autistic individuals are far more likely than allistics to experience adverse events and traumatic experiences, while also less likely to be diagnosed with or treated for the traumatic stress they experience. Interestingly, this higher rate of trauma isn't solely due to autistic individuals being easier to victimize; population data demonstrates that autistic children are also exposed to significantly more trauma in the form of familial divorce, parents with substance use problems and/or mental illness, neighborhood violence, and poverty. There are many possible reasons why these numbers are so high; the disparity is very likely due to multiple factors.

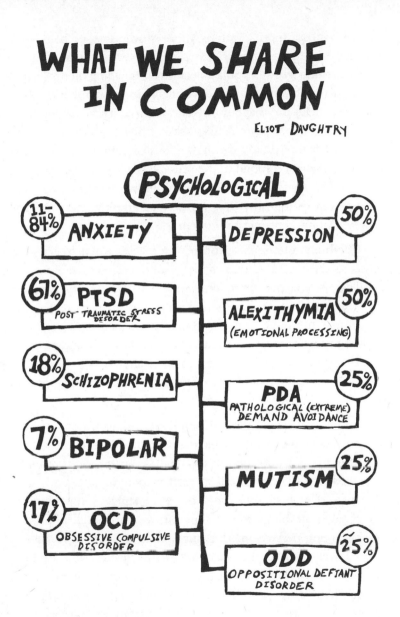

The autistic brain both is more susceptible to being taken advantage of and has trouble noticing larger patterns, so autistic people are doubly susceptible to trauma misleading them. That raw data from our brain is not made available to our conscious selves—only the conclusions that our brain draws from it are. Interpretations of that data inform our reality—sometimes inaccurately. If your worldview is interpreted through a lens of unhealed trauma, you are more likely to respond to the present as if you are reliving a past trauma. One study linked instances of autistic people being violent to instances of unresolved past traumas. Frankly, this is probably why neurotypical people are violent too.

The human brain is a storytelling machine that tries to make sense of the world. Understanding someone else's sense-making is called an "enactive approach." So let's use an enactive approach to understand how trauma works for an autistic person. The three features of the brain that likely play the biggest role in why an autistic person is more susceptible to trauma reactions are a lower neurological threshold, differences in ability to self-regulate, and differences in sense-making. Let's look at what these things mean in relation to adverse events.

- *Neurological threshold* is the limit of a person's ability to process and tolerate sensory stimuli. We each have a threshold for information our bodies can take in through the senses. There is only a certain amount of sounds in our ears, sights in our range of vision, smells, temperature changes, or things on our skin that we can handle without becoming overwhelmed. Autistic individuals tend to have a lower neurological threshold than allistics, at least in some areas. While increasing some sensory stimuli may be soothing (a weighted blanket, thumping bass music), those sensations are being used to block out other sensations or calm a nervous system that has become overloaded from other input.

- *Self-regulation and sense-making* are exactly what they sound like: our ability to moderate our nervous systems in any given situation (especially difficult ones) and our ability to make sense of the world. These are skills that are partially innate in humans and are learned and curated further as we mature and grow. These systems work differently among neurodivergent people. And it isn't just as simple an answer as *it's harder*. The fact that *it's different* is enough. If the allistics around you have an agreed-upon, shared reality of an event and you don't see it that way? You now may feel confused, rejected, anxious, isolated, and detached and find yourself questioning everything about yourself.

If our trauma responses are more about how we process a traumatic event and the support we have in healing and recovery (or lack thereof), it makes sense that an autistic person would be more susceptible to traumatic stress—both from things that everyone would agree are traumatic and from things that many people wouldn't even think about that way. One study surveyed autistic people, assessing them both for what the *DSM-5* considers a traumatic event that results in PTSD and also for what the autistic people found to be traumatic. The answers were heartbreaking. Many people struggled with bullying, abandonment by family members, grief, their own mental health struggles, and the autism spectrum disorder (ASD) diagnostic process itself.

And now that we have some better understanding of how an autistic person sees the world (through practicing our enactive approach), it becomes very obvious why these issues could easily be experienced as traumatic stress. And if you don't have the support you need, this can turn into PTSD.

So when we discuss the high instances of depression and anxiety among autistic people that we talked about in the diagnosis section, we have to think about how traumatic stress may influence these conditions. One study demonstrated that 90% of individuals diagnosed with both ASD and a mood disorder had a significant trauma history. Of the autistic individuals with no co-occurring mood disorder, 40% had a trauma history.

Part of managing the effects of trauma is recognizing that allistic people are unreliable narrators about the facts of their own experiences. Allistics don't care about the action; they care about the meaning they find in that action. Which, in the case of trauma, often means being triggered by things that others wouldn't notice. Read *The Invisible Gorilla* by Christopher Chabris and Daniel Simons if you aren't familiar with the research in that domain. A person's sensors become too subjectively attuned, and the allistic brain is more likely to remember the emotional experience of how something felt, rather than the material facts of what happened. Accepting this can be very difficult because your reality is so convincing. When others disagree, it can feel like they are trying to overwrite our emotional experiences with their own.

Maybe your reading about trauma makes you think less about your partner and more "it me," and you're probably right. Trauma is a normal human experience, and it can really screw up our ability to live calm and connected lives. The good news is that you can totally heal—and one of the ways we can get better is by being in a loving and secure relationship.

FUNCTIONING VS. COPING

We already said it, but it's worth saying again: there is no distinction between "high-functioning" and "low-functioning" variations of autism.[10]

"Low functioning" is a phrase coined in the 1980s to describe autistic kids that also had an IQ below 70. Over time, use of "low functioning" was twisted and distorted to apply not just to someone's intellectual capacity, but also to their development timeline. While IQ measures a person's critical understanding of select items prioritized by upper-class white people, development refers to how someone matures in relation to their biological age. The dichotomy of high/low functioning is misleading and often becomes self-fulfilling through self-image.

The myth is that the *Rain Man* savant doing calculus while staring into the carpet, incapable of communicating verbally, is "low functioning." But as we invest in more research around neurodiversity, it's clear that this is a false narrative. In those moments, you are witnessing an overwhelmed autist who is incapable of accessing their social skills. When autistics blend into mixed environments, society refers to them as "high functioning," questioning whether they are autistic at all. Autistic women in particular are often raised to be more adept at coping with—and thus hiding—their differences and social confusion. They carefully observe others and learn intellectually how to pass sometimes as an allistic, however briefly. These people are performing incredible amounts of emotional labor to perform allistic normalcy. Inevitably, they will eventually exhaust

10 Don't just take our word for it: the high- vs. low-functioning distinction no longer exists in the *DSM-5*. Many people continue to use it in daily conversation, but for over a decade now, the clinical position has been to instead talk about "support needs," which is helpful information; functioning level, meanwhile, is as random and unhelpful as the *DSM* GAF (Global Assessment of Functioning), which applied to all diagnostic impressions and which we also no longer use.

themselves and need time to decompress. In those moments they will bear little resemblance to their public selves, and you might refer to them as "low functioning." At times, Joe has been nonverbal for weeks or months when it's just been too overwhelming to form ideas into words.

Researchers at five universities tracked 400 autistic children for 15 years after their autism diagnosis. The researchers watched as their autistic symptoms and functionality changed over the years. Kids who had been labeled "low functioning" were suddenly "high functioning" in some situations, and vice versa. It now seemed like these functioning labels were products of an allistic bias and an incomplete understanding of autism.

According to another study performed by Gail Alvares, PhD, and colleagues, a person with "high-functioning" autism is not any higher functioning than someone with "low-functioning" autism. Further, studies for IQ have long been found to be rooted in racism, so much so that courts found it unlawful to test IQs in Black students in California. By their nature, IQ tests are studying a person's cultural

Has developed a set of healthy coping skills

Can endure stressful situations sometimes. Deemed "high functioning"

Not managing maladaptive responses to trauma and abuse

experiences rather than their intelligence. This raises an important question: If IQ is biased towards allistic experiences (similarly to how it's biased in other ways), how can it purport to measure the capabilities of an autistic person?

An autistic person's level of functioning is a product of their learned ability to develop helpful coping skills when they find a situation overwhelming. So instead of judging your partner's functionality, talk about it. Ask them questions to learn about what helps them cope in each situation where they become overwhelmed. Doing so increases their abilities instead of limiting their potential.

Example? I (Faith) have a lovely and brilliant friend from the same Indigenous nation to which I belong. My friend has a master's degree, is working on a PhD, and speaks several languages. They are also an autist. During the middle of a medical crisis recently, speaking became more and more difficult for him because of the overwhelm He eventually switched back to his first language, Choctaw, to communicate with me. For all humans, our first language is our emotional language (which is why being able to do therapy in this language is so helpful), so it was easier for them to express their fear and overwhelm. Plus the structure and syntax rules for Choctaw are both simpler and more specific (e.g., we don't have a plural form: it's not helpful to say you have cats; instead, say you have 1 cat or 37 cat or too many cat to even count). Everyone at the hospital he was staying in likely considered him low functioning. To me, this linguistic switch was exceptional functioning because it helped him manage his own brain while sharing with me.

Many parents of autistic children set very low expectations for their kids. Inevitably, the kids cannot find motivation and struggle to achieve independence, living down to those low expectations. This is, again, due to the focus on making allistics comfortable around autistic people rather than building a set of life skills for the autistic person to achieve independence. In one case, a parent touted it as a great success that her autistic son didn't have a meltdown during Christmas dinner, even though his every need and whim needed to be attended to by someone else. These low expectations often stem in part from misunderstanding or mismanagement of meltdowns.

A meltdown is when someone cannot access their coping skills and the overwhelm boils over into a sudden rage and forces them to take a break. This might involve screaming. Sometimes, when Joe has a meltdown, it feels like melting through the floor to depart the situation (flight); in reality, it's a loss of control, and it typically involves crying helplessly, going silent—almost catatonic (freeze)—or having what appears to be a temper tantrum (fight). Meltdowns may look different for different people, so talk with your partner to learn their signs and what they need.

It's important to understand some of the causes of meltdowns. For one thing, it's very difficult for autistic people to have crushed expectations, so it can be helpful to develop ways to prevent this from happening. Just like chafing clothing can cause overwhelm, so can repeating a situation that was fun the first time but crippling the next due to a factor like overcrowding or too much sunlight. A certain amount of predictability can be established in daily life, but we need to have safeguards for moments like when we get locked out of the house or get on the wrong bus.

Meltdowns are more controllable as we get older. Once we hit our mid to late 20s, our prefrontal cortex is fully developed, which helps a ton. A young autistic person unloads immediately. Early adult meltdowns involve a burst of anger, banging of the head against the wall, emotional/physical shutdown, obsessive behavior, or other stress relief. But as autistic people age, the meltdowns tend to happen when they have space and time for them, and they're also more likely to experience a shutdown instead. For instance, nowadays, at the end of a long day, Joe gets a headache and retires to bed in the afternoon to watch TV. Similarly, Joe gets sick after getting home from every trip.

During meltdowns and shutdowns, autistic people become unreachable. And it's worth remembering that, regardless of how you feel as a witness, your partner is likely overwhelmed, upset, embarrassed, and shocked by their own behavior. It's best to talk about it the next day, when the intense feelings and overwhelm have faded and before it contributes to clinical depression.

EMPATHY AND EMOTIONS

Joe here. Your partner may have trouble with empathy and emotions, but maybe not in the way you assume. Sometimes we feel so much empathy that it is deafening. Other times we cannot understand someone else's experience, so we feel nothing about it. Sometimes things that are really upsetting for others have no apparent impact on us. This is okay, but it's what leads allistics to pathologize us as sociopaths. Researcher Simon Baron-Cohen has depicted autistic people as largely devoid of empathy, further setting back popular understanding of our internal experience. Building upon this limited understanding, researchers Robert Schultz, Coralie Chevallier, and Gregor Kohls have written that autistic children might not feel as "rewarded" by the act of engaging with others as allistics do, making us less motivated and, over time, less able to see the internal experiences of others. But this also means that when we *are* motivated, we are quite capable of empathy and do it "unexpectedly" well. Why is that unexpected? Because allistics have a very difficult time understanding lived experiences outside of their own. In a more recent study, autistic people were found to have an equal ability to recognize regret and relief as compared to allistics. Individual mileage with empathy may vary, however.

Let's break down autistic empathy and emotional intelligence.

- *Autistic people have emotions. So many emotions.* Sometimes it can be difficult to detect expressions of emotions from your partner because they don't come across in the way that you are used to. When I'm sad, rather than demonstrating facial expressions, I become quiet and offer bare-minimum responses to questions. I'm quickly overwhelmed, so I avoid eye contact, and sometimes there is crying involved. Like all things for autistic people, my experiences and expressions are roughly 42% exaggerated.[11]

- *Autistic people have empathy; too much empathy.* Once, getting off a plane, I accidentally elbowed a stranger in the face and immediately associated it with feeling pain. I had a rush of feelings and *excessively* apologized. However, at the same time, when I say something that people find grating or insulting, it's more difficult for me to realize it unless they say something. Often, what feels insulting is very confusing. The other day I was talking about a TV show that I enjoyed, and the other person said that their parents enjoyed it too; the person felt insulted when I said that the show felt like it was written for children—even though I enjoyed the same show, this statement felt diminishing of their parents' interests. I guess I just don't have the skills to realize how something might be taken as insulting. Part of the reason for this is brain wiring. There are two different kinds of empathy: affective empathy is the instinctive ability to experience others' emotions like a contagious disease, while cognitive empathy is the conscious drive

11 4200% might be more realistic, but scientific study is still pending

to recognize someone else's emotional state based on their speech, behavior, and nonverbal communication. A sociopath often has a low level of affective empathy and a high level of cognitive empathy, meaning that they know what is the correct response and how to exploit it without actually experiencing it. An autistic person tends to have the opposite configuration: a low level of cognitive ability to recognize others' experience but an extreme, visceral reaction to it when we understand what's going on. By relating your experiences back to our own, we can tap into our affective empathy to feel your pain and become invested in preventing similar things from happening again. You can therefore create shorthand expressions to remind your partner how to relate their own behavior to others' lived experiences. For example, "Remember the time so-and-so said this about you and it wasn't true so you were confused and hurt? That's how I feel right now."

- *Autistic people need to off-load as an alternate method of preventing overwhelm.* My hobby is observing inappropriate overheards in public. It's a detached way to learn and practice social skills while also mastering a comedy routine! And it's tremendously amusing to observe how allistics do not follow their own social rules but then complain when autistics don't. However, when I post these observances on social media, allistics tend to respond with empathy for me instead of amusement. Silly allistics.

- *One thing that offends autistic people above all is injustice.* Our empathy is more global than localized to our immediate environment. It's easier to relate with an animal species across the planet or a complicated social problem than with somebody getting fired from a job for poor performance or having a complicated travel experience. We are trying to be helpful by being logical or offering unsolicited advice . . . even though that's probably not what you are looking for. Our efforts in these social arenas are often awkward. If you explain this to us—what our clumsy efforts at empathy feel like and what is wanted instead—you can eradicate these encounters and replace them with clear instructions for what feels good for both of you. Helping others is hugely rewarding and motivating for us, so if you frame your needs in that way, it can create a win-win.

- *Autistic people are not typically sociopaths. We do not habitually practice coercive control.* A friend who was dating an autistic woman told me that he ran into a flyer at his college warning about the dangers of abusive relationships. The flyer depicted his partner's behavior to a T: "Does your partner have concerns about what you wear, your schedule, your activities, even your phone usage?" Now this is a common blurring of the lines for autistic people: confusing or conflating us with abusers. The one fundamental difference is that we aren't trying to reduce you to our low level of self-esteem or control you. We are merely very particular about maintaining control over our own environments in an effort to preserve our own sanity and longevity. Yes, plenty of autistic people *have* developed maladaptive coping mechanisms that lead to conflict, hostility, and confrontation, and it's possible that through this maladaptive behavior, autistic people may find that demanding that others do their bidding can get their needs met. But this is a bug, not a feature, and maladaptive coping mechanisms tend to go away eventually in healthy relationships with firm boundaries, as the autistic partner gets their needs met in other ways. Autistic partners also tend to respect boundaries more quickly than allistics, so long as the boundaries are clearly and concretely stated. Parsing through all of this may feel like splitting hairs at times. In these moments, if you are concerned that you are being abused, ask yourself, "Is my partner unnecessarily escalating, or are they expressing an unfulfilled need?" Sometimes it's important to walk your partner back from the ledge. What are they trying to achieve? Are they achieving what they set out to? Is there a better way to get there together?

- *Autistic people don't usually know how to flirt or cheat.* Though that doesn't prevent the opposite appearance from taking shape in our partners' minds. While research demonstrates that humans are, by and large, non-monogamous by nature, and some people act on the urge to step out of their monogamy agreement, that impulse is generally not acted on by autistic people. Autistic people are loyal even when it's illogical to be, as when our partners have proven their own lack of loyalty. We are also more comfortable becoming friends with our exes, though that is not always popular behavior with our current partner.

- *Autistic people do more emotional and relational labor than allistics because we exist in a world built for neurotypicals.* If we are going to survive, we simply have to do more emotional labor. This is partly through masking, which we do to make allistics more comfortable, and partly through having to do so much extra work to unpack and understand everything happening around us. We need to make up for the instinctual privileges that more than 98% of the population is born with and intellectually overcome our neurological differences. We are constantly needing to regulate our feelings in order to fit into every situation. By thinking about things that most people take for granted all day long, we question assumptions and arrive at our own creative conclusions. As we enter adulthood, we need to understand the relational dynamics and feelings of people around us. This means listening closely and talking about what we experience, checking in frequently with people that we care about, and asking thoughtful, direct questions about how people would like to be treated. Constant personal growth is a must for us, and we continue it throughout our entire lives, long after others stagnate into habits.

• *Autistic people's ability to act is not impeded by emotions, except in cases of meltdown.* When allistics are overwhelmed and disabled by their emotions, autistic people remain plodding along, successfully completing one task at a time. We bring a new perspective that helps you see your problems differently. We find the solutions that others cannot see.

Emotional growth is hard, and autistic people who came up in an ableist society may have a harder time than most. But it's also worth considering that as an allistic person you may be the one at a disadvantage, since there is much you may be accustomed to taking for granted rather than having to figure out from scratch. Understanding where emotions come from and how to manage them is not something you can do for your partner, but you can do it for yourself and support each other along the way.

EXECUTIVE FUNCTION

Autistic people are great at things that most people can't do, but at the same time, it can be hard for them to manage things that other people do easily. Executive functioning (EF) is one of the things that doesn't come naturally to them. Executive functions are the processes by which we can exhibit control and goal-directed behaviors. These processes include working memory (how much current information we can hold and process), urge control (this is not just behavioral, but also involves recognizing whether thoughts and feelings are accurate or brain trash), and flexible thinking (our ability to look at problems and solutions from different angles).

Whether the goal is mailing a letter, getting a job, or getting elected president, the better someone is at EF, the more likely they are to achieve it. And "non-normative" EF is one of the hallmarks of autism, just as it is with other forms of neurodivergence. One might say this commonality explains why diagnoses like ADHD and OCD ended up co-occurring with autism.

So your autistic partner might have big plans but struggle mightily to get them done, or even to know where to begin. Or they might just get frustrated trying to do everyday tasks like cooking or grocery shopping. Or maybe they've figured out ways to be great or just get by in a number of domains, but they lose it when trying to add something new or when there's a change in routine.

EF problems can also lead to time blindness, which often creates anxiety about time. If your partner doesn't enjoy a task, they may have no knowledge of whether it takes two minutes or two hours. They might operate on their own time entirely, or they might be obsessed with arriving exactly on time, or arriving exactly five minutes early, in order to have time to calm down or perform other rituals to resituate in their body. Understanding what they need is far more important than understanding why they need it, and the most important thing is not imposing how you do things or what you think is best for them.

Joe here. It's also important to understand that, especially in professional life, EF is tied to discrimination. Periodically I find myself in a place full of people where no one will talk to me. I try to spark conversation but people don't want to engage. Sometimes I apply for a job, contract, or speaking gig and have qualifications that exceed the requirements, but someone less qualified is hired instead. Most opportunities are social in nature, and I cannot see how others see me. The issue stems from a combination of social discrimination and not being able to build towards a goal. I know many autistic people who are high performers at work but are continually passed over for promotions, simply because they lack the intangible, unearned confidence of the ascending executive. For a job interviewer, my manner of speaking and appearance carry more weight than my skills or abilities. Conversely, I cannot see the "bad optics" of my amalgamated choices. In short, I look like a sloppy mess who is a bit of a loose cannon or wild card. I cannot see this because I see each of my choices as separate, individual things rather than as the composite that they create. On rare occasions, I ask someone what happened and they point out a series of very specific and seemingly irrelevant things that I did and said. They explain to me that these things are immature and that other people notice these patterns and make judgments about me as a result. Sometimes these polite, patient people also explain to me how my composite choices actually drive me *away* from my goals.

EF can be learned; your partner having trouble with it now doesn't mean they always will.[12] But be warned that EF problems

12 EF can be improved through practice, especially when this is done with intentionality. Faith tells clients regularly that the brain needs two things to be healthy: meditation and frustration. Meditation is how we stop and notice our own internal processes, and frustration means taking on a complex task, struggling a bit, then figuring out the solution. Brains loooooooove a good problem to solve, and this is how EF skills are built. It isn't enough to just use what we have; we have to grow past what is already there. This is how we build new neural pathways and

can lead to one of the most pernicious relationship difficulties in interabled relationships: you may be tempted to take control of life's logistics for your partner (or you may already have a long-standing habit of doing so). Even if it is not your intent and your partner doesn't read it that way, over time you are in danger of creating a dynamic in which you are treating your partner like a child, assigning them tasks and reminding them constantly to complete them—or, worse, blowing up at them when they don't. You can support and encourage their growth and goals in many other ways without taking on this role for them.

SPECIAL INTERESTS

One of the stereotypical traits of autism is to have a special interest that verges on obsession. These interests can be more or less socially acceptable.

You might be familiar with *Rain Man* or *The Big Bang Theory*, which convinced the world that if someone were *really* autistic, they would be lying facedown on the floor performing experimental calculus equations in their head or loudly prattling on about some eccentric topic for your entertainment. Of course, neither of these are terribly accurate portrayals of real people; they are exaggerations of autistic personality traits.

On the other hand, neither of these depictions are entirely wrong. Autistic people do tend to be obsessed with things. You might have read about the autistic man so obsessed with trains and buses that he steals them from New York City and pilots them across state

strengthen our abilities in this area. And no, you don't have to go to one of those brain-training gyms or use one of those apps to get results; there are lots of ways to incorporate EF training into one's regular, daily environment. The website for *ADDitude* magazine has an article entitled "How to Sharpen Executive Functions: Activities to Hone Brain Skills," which is a great starting point for ideas.

lines. When I (Joe) was making my first feature film, I would spend days in the editing studio, to the point that I depleted my physical health. My hyperfocus was pulling me into the project to the degree that I could work overnights without sleeping. I would forget to eat because I was so focused on what I was doing. Only because my date had requested it, I would walk to a pay phone to call her every 10 hours to relay that yes, I was still working. But it didn't feel like work to me. It was all that I could think about. The immersive obsession had unexpected benefits: for example, the long days of intensive video editing showed me for the first time that people's emotions are displayed in their facial expressions. However, there were also drawbacks. As one woman that I worked with put it, "Joe dragged their body around for years until it couldn't be dragged anymore." Our interests speak louder to us than any other force in the world.

As in any relationship, supporting your partner's interests is awesome. This doesn't mean they have to become your interests too; you can carve out time to talk about other things. We talk more about this in the connection section in chapter 3.

Beving "obsessed" with things can be healthy to a certain extent; there is nothing wrong with getting excited about stuff unless it keeps us from caring for our lives in other important ways (as in the case of the obsessive film editing). But we can get carried away into unhealthy territory if we get obsessed with a *person* instead of *things*. This can result in serious boundary violations, such as stalking, that can get us into real trouble in addition to freaking out the people that we care about. As a teenager, I met a friend for coffee every day. When she didn't show up one day, I went to her house, where she was still sleeping. Because these routines weren't explicit—even though they felt that way for me—my appearance at her house felt invasive and creepy for her. It's possible that your partner might fixate on you as one of their special interests, especially if they don't have a lot of past relationship experience. In these cases, explicating what makes a behavior a problem and setting a specific boundary will put us on a much happier, healthier, and safer course.

There is also some common confusion about the supposed similarity between autistics and people with OCD. The difference between an autistic person and someone with OCD is that autistic people don't believe that our obsessive habits are unreasonable and can explain the benefits of them. We can change our behavior and, unless we are overwhelmed by anxiety, depression, and trauma, we can largely choose our actions.

SENSORY ISSUES

Joe again. Stimulus and sensory issues are often an enormous struggle for us. That is to say, light, sound, touch, smell, or taste that is unnoticeable or even positive for allistics may be unpleasant or overwhelming for us. Conversely, an autistic person may also need a greater sensation to produce the same effect as in an allistic person, like stronger flavors in food or a firmer touch—romantically or in a massage—to feel good. What we often consider a sensory processing issue is better thought of as a sensory integration issue. We are processing sensory input just fine; we just can't integrate it into our perception of the world at the moment without feeling attacked by things that aren't actually dangerous. Sensory input will activate the body's stress response system with a flood of hormones.

This connects with our earlier statement that, for autistics, everything is 42% more overwhelming. We see more, hear more, feel more, smell more, and taste more than allistic people. For example, eye contact contains too much information and can be painful. Sooner or later, these things add up and become overwhelming. And we can't turn it off. Our brain doesn't sort through all that sensory input and ignore all but the most important, like allistic brains do. That's why, for example, autistic people usually cut the tags out of our clothes, and wearing very comfortable clothes is more important to us than fashion. Because if we have a tag tickling us or are wearing a shirt that is slightly itchy, our brain won't ignore it after a while like yours does; we will just keep feeling it every minute, all day long. The autistic brain is constantly making computations and calculations, which we cannot stop.

Autistic people also frequently experience synesthesia, a phenomenon where one kind of sensory input is perceived through another sense entirely. Sometimes we have mixed inputs from overwhelm that cause us to taste colors and hear food (while some foods do make noise, sound isn't typically the primary way people process different kinds of food; but for those with synesthesia, it might be). Autistic brains cannot interpret the multitude of sensory inputs into something to respond to, and we want consistency above all.

Keep in mind, though, that each person's sensory needs are different. For example, I like to eat foods with a lot of complex, strong flavors, which is not true for all autistic people. But when Elly is cooking in the slow cooker, the smells that she finds pleasant are so unpleasant to me that I have to leave the house for hours.

Sensory issues can take over our lives and affect all our relationships. When I was a member of an autistic social group and the group walked outside together to go home, nearly everyone would make use of noise-canceling headphones, sunglasses, parasols, and broad-brimmed hats. The sunlight and noise from the outdoors would cause headaches, overwhelm, and nausea in almost everyone. When the sunlight comes into my office, I am incapable of focusing. A hug or other contact that is intended to be a pleasant sensation can be quite unpleasant and even traumatic due to pressure, texture, or moisture that overwhelms our senses. Even the feel of water or soap can be dramatically unpleasant to the touch. There were years of my life when I was not comfortable wearing clothes—whatsoever—and I don't think this is atypical.[13] The sound of silverware scratching a pot or other silverware feels physically painful inside of me.

We don't always hear our name being called if we are hyperfocused on something else that we are listening to. Our capacity for new information is limited, so we often have to choose what to subject ourselves to or else suffer overwhelm. Think of this like spoons[14]—you only have so many. For example, it's easier to listen to someone when I am looking at the floor. There are fewer stimulus units. When I reached overwhelm as an adult before my diagnosis, I would just adopt a dissociative blank stare and need some time to re-enter the moment. Now I'm a bit better at pacing and moderating my stimulus so that I don't reach that point.

Due to these sensory sensitivities, we are notoriously picky eaters. Wanting to be certain of how a food will taste, for example, might lead an autistic person to choose Oreos over grapes. Oreos *always* taste the same. Grapes may be delicious, and firm, and sweet . . . or they could be sour or squishy or something that tastes or feels awful to someone with sensory sensitivities.

Faith here. Autistic people can sometimes develop "feeding disorders," which are talked about much less than eating disorders but are far more common than most clinicians realize. While there is enough overlap between the two that both are listed in the same category in the *DSM-5*, eating disorders are developed as a coping

13 Faith agrees. Her oldest was allowed to be a nekkie baby at home so long as they didn't strip in the middle of the grocery store. The plan worked well, for the most part.

14 The spoon theory is a concept thought up by Christine Miserandino to explain how those living with chronic illness or disabilities must make difficult decisions about how to expend their limited energy. Imagine all your energy at the beginning of the day as a finite collection of spoons. Each thing you do— from getting up and dressed to having a conversation to walking to the store—takes a certain number of spoons, and you have to figure out how to budget them.

skill for emotional pain, whereas feeding disorders are a direct result of food intolerances and strong food preferences. The treatment for feeding disorders is to help find the individual food or foods that the person can tolerate. I once chatted with the concerned parent of an autistic teen who thought he was parenting poorly by buying them milkshakes constantly. But the milkshakes went down just fine and the child needed nutrients. You wouldn't fuss over someone getting over being sick or going through chemo who could only tolerate certain foods, right? While it's not appropriate to parent our partners, it's important to understand the adult decisions of your autistic partner through this lens. They are getting their needs met through methods that help them survive and be healthy, even if those methods might not hold up to the scrutiny of country club folks. So instead of judging your partner's choices based on what you would do or even what makes sense to you, ask, "Is this choice helping them or harming them?" and withhold judgment or discuss your concerns with them, as appropriate.

My own neurodivergent kiddo grew up with the same "courtesy bite" rule as their allistic brother. People are allowed to not like stuff and shouldn't be forced to clean their plate, but I did want my kiddo to try new things. So they had to try one bite. If they didn't like it, no more was required; but if they did, they could have more. No power struggles ever took place under this system, and both kids ended up liking and eating far more interesting foods than they would have if they had fights at every meal that wasn't chicky nuggies.

STIMMING

Nutrition, exercise, and the like help mitigate the body's stress response to sensory input, but only somewhat. Hence, stimming is the body's physiological response to an overstimulated nervous system—a way to throw off all of the extra energy.

Joe here. When we are overwhelmed, we fall into fight, flight, or freeze, caused by HPA axis dysregulation. This is where stimming calms us down. It can take the form of touching a certain texture, rubbing or flapping our hands, rocking in place, rubbing our hair, making repeated gestures or sounds, spinning a coin, playing with a fidget spinner, organizing our environments, or otherwise getting our bearings and moving ourselves back to the present. We do this to feel control within our environment.

When I was a child, I "cleaned up" my Legos every day by organizing them into a row—a way of engaging in stimming through organizing my environment. This was comforting to me, but psychologists call such behaviors "purposeless," because apparently comfort isn't a purpose.[15] I also spent hours feeling the texture of a torn-up, dirty blanket. It brought comfort to my small, chaotic world. Naturally, it was destroyed in the washing machine when my neighbors got lice. As we enter adulthood, stimming tends to take the form of foot tapping or other subtle maneuvers. Nowadays, I instinctively say the name of my dog or play with my hair or rub my fingers together. These kinds of behaviors—along with playing with toys, drumming our fingers, or bending paper clips—are more socially acceptable than flapping our hands.

Ironically, stimming is less socially acceptable than coping mechanisms that are much more harmful. Not convinced? Go to a bar and watch how socially acceptable drinking is. Still not convinced? Go on the internet and look at how much of online discourse involves comforting strangers by saying that other people are "garbage." Consider how all of this coping affects other people and how harmless yet socially unacceptable stimming is. And by the

15 Jokes aside, the reason that autistic comfort is deemed "purposeless" is because psychology is more interested in allistic comfort and the status quo than the comfort of autistic people. This is an example of ableism in the framework. It doesn't make sense to allistic psychologists; thus they conclude that it doesn't serve a purpose.

way, if you think allistics don't stim, go to a rock concert and watch how suddenly everyone moves to the music like an autistic person.

If your partner is stimming in private or in public, they are trying to calm themselves. Comfort them subtly and ask how they are feeling or if you can do anything to help. The allistic tendency is to try and stop them, but this will only make their problem worse. Stimming serves an important purpose in nervous system regulation. Trying to suppress this behavior has been correlated with an increase in psychological harm. Never take away helpful or neutral coping mechanisms; let the stimming happen. If you notice it causing problems with outside people, bring it up. Your partner can take the information you give them and decide whether or not to change their stimming habits.

MASKING

Masking is the stressful act of performing neurotypicality and hiding one's autism by acting allistic. This might involve developing a public persona to show the world, or it might involve trying to create a separate persona for each interaction based on a perception of what each person wants to see. Masking is taught as part of applied behavior analysis (ABA), the popular methodology used to try to "fix" the behavior of autistic children through molding their expression to make the allistic world more comfortable. ABA therapy is widespread even though it is so stressful that it actually decreases a sense of belonging and leads to suicidality in many cases. Still, for most autistic people, the only consideration in regards to masking is whether it's more burdensome to mask or to suffer worse treatment for the sin of being themselves in a given situation.

In some cases, masking serves as a strength as long as the emotional cost is mitigated. Autistic people assume roles well.

Performing is easier for them, whether the performance is taking place in a relationship, at parties, at work, or onstage. Autistic adults have a lifetime of practice masking their behaviors in order to master self-preservation and avoidance. After a lifetime of bullying, they work to blend in, so you likely won't even notice their differences until a few awkward moments of miscommunication transpire. This is why, as children, they attempt to be social chameleons and stick to solitary interests in things like animals and fiction. As autistic people get older, performing a role becomes easier than being authentically themselves, because it offers a path that is singular and clear. Autistic people naturally imitate and adopt personas and characters both as a way of being accepted and as a way of interfacing with ideas. Performing roles results in clearer behavior, rewards, and positions for everyone. Most allistics can't interpret the facial expressions or mannerisms of autistic people and vice versa. Theatrical performance, which is essentially what masking is, is a language that bridges that gap.

Autistic people often find themselves in a double bind: they can mask hard and appear neurotypical, in which case they won't be believed when they need support; or they can appear to be a total mess, in which case they will be deemed incapable of functioning independently altogether—versus just, you know, being asked what they need and how they are looking to grow as people.

Your partner may be so adept at masking that they don't even realize that they do it, and letting their guard down in front of others, including you, might feel very vulnerable for them. The better you know them, the easier it will be to tell when they're masking and how much it takes out of them and to show them that you will continue to love, accept, and listen to them just as well, regardless of how they are managing their tone, facial expressions, eye contact, and body language.

GENDER IDENTITY AND SEXUALITY

It's highly probable that your autistic partner is some flavor of queer and/or transgender, whether or not they or you are currently aware of this. This isn't an inherent feature of autism—there are plenty of cis, straight autistics out there—but it's such a common experience that we wanted to talk about it.

I (Joe) am not cisgender, don't use pronouns, and tried—for a time—to convince others to stop gendering me. However, it became more exhausting to correct people than to let it pass. Fundamentally, I want people to respect me and where I'm coming from, not recite facts back to me. I found that I was only pushed further into the margins whenever I corrected someone about my gender. Correcting people incessantly only further isolates me, causes me to lose ground and respect, and takes away from any point that I am trying to make. Of course, this is not the case for everyone; your partner may find that correcting others who misgender them is important for establishing their identity and self-respect.

There hasn't been sufficient study about the overlap of ASD and sexual/gender minorities, so we don't definitively know how big the overlap is. Apparently science has done a very bad job of studying this, because research indicates that the figure is anywhere from 4% to 69% of autistic people are sexual/gender minorities—a spread big enough to be functionally useless. Studies vary in rigor, and many use only a screening tool rather than a full assessment to "diagnose" autism. There are no real answers yet.

So let's focus on what we know, much of which is based on personal observations. Around 90% of autistic people under 30 that I have met are not cisgender. Among autistic people under 40 that I know, the figure is 70%. The numbers continue in this trajectory as the age groups get older, and this seems to be about self-awareness and the cultural freedom to express yourself, which wasn't available to older generations. (You know. Boomers.) One study found that 70% of autistic people are not heterosexual. This may have something to do with the fact that taboos and shame are merely less obstructive of the true desires of autistic people because we say what we mean.

Gender identity becomes so wrapped up in autistic identity that the term "autigender" has been created to describe this growing group of autists. The strange thing is that, perhaps since we are an emerging group during a series of culture wars, many trans people will tell us that we aren't "really" trans, that this is just us being weird, that it's an "autistic perseveration," or that we're trying to glom on to another emergent trend. Queer people are protective of their communities because they have been under attack for centuries. Still, it can be rather exhausting to carve out your own space and have to defend it from other marginalized people who are afraid that you are trying to claim a piece of their pie.

Having a number of intersecting marginalized identities also means more opportunities for discrimination and othering at work, in public, with family, and in social situations. In the last chapter of this book we have advice for supporting and advocating for your partner around others. Here, we will focus on how to support your partner within your relationship.

Supporting a partner who is coming out as a sexual or gender minority is similar to supporting a partner who is coming out as autistic (which we will also cover in more detail later on). Believe them, support them, and remember that they are still the same person you fell in love with. Read up, and ask them questions about their experiences and wishes. Bear with them as their own self-understanding evolves rapidly, and stand by them when they face discrimination and harassment. Think of this exploration as similar to them having a new job—you want to hear about it, and you'll be there for the ups and downs, but you can't do the work for them. When they first start to come out, check in from time to time about whether there are any changes in how they want to be supported. For instance, they might start out by wanting you to use their new pronouns (or lack thereof) but not wanting you to correct others who get it wrong. Over time, they may change how they want you to refer to them and how they want you to handle interactions with different people in different situations. It may be helpful for your partner to work with a therapist who specializes in gender so they can disambiguate these identities safely and do some discernment work without judgment (for further discussion about therapy, see chapter 3).

The world is already really, really hard. Let's not create more problems. We need to listen to people's lived experience and respect the domain of their bodies. If someone wants to transition, it's not hurting anybody, and it's not our place to be judgmental or critical of that need. We don't need so many checkpoints for care; gender affirming medical interventions are based on informed consent. Talk to your partner about how they would like to manage their gender identity. Then, with that information, advocate for what they need.

CHAPTER 2:
YOUR ALLISTIC PERSPECTIVE

*T*he last chapter was about understanding your partner. This chapter is about understanding *your* role, your expectations, your privileges (and the power inherent in them), and what your partner probably needs most from you.

Elly here. Joe and I got together about a year before Joe's diagnosis. I had made the decision early on in our relationship to accept Joe at face value, exactly as is. I decided to trust Joe's motives and believe Joe's words, rather than looking for hidden meanings and agendas. Joe's qualities include incredible intelligence and vision, a sense of humor that leaves me roaring helplessly with laughter daily, loyalty and determination in epic proportions, and the ability to carry absolutely anything found on the side of the road across town on a bicycle and then build bookcases out of it. At the time we started dating, this list also included alarming accident-proneness, the social fallout from past failed relationships, literal and figurative fires, and a lot of last-minute scrambling to (successfully!) execute grand, incompletely planned projects.

I was attracted to Joe's uniqueness, direct way of asking questions and communicating about emotional topics, and ability to think, see, and do in ways that regularly blew my mind. Joe was the first person in my life to ever ask me what my needs were in a relationship, and to be able to state their own in turn. I was also (I can say now with years of therapy under my belt) attracted to the chaotic state of Joe's life at the time. I was never bored: there was always some adventure, crisis, or exciting problem to solve! I'm not sure we would have gotten together if Joe had already been diagnosed and adjusted to that diagnosis—in that alternate universe,

I doubt I would have been enticed by the stability. Praise math we grew in that direction together.

Witnessing Joe figure out how to live more easily in the world post-diagnosis has been a privilege, and it's made room for our relationship to deepen and grow in healthy ways. But I definitely had some learning and even more unlearning to do, especially in the ways that I had stepped up—and Joe was complicit in this as well—to smooth over the rough places where I sensed Joe was out of sync with the world. What Joe learned post-diagnosis made much of this stepping up obsolete, but it took longer for me to catch up. It was like I'd gotten so used to applying pressure to a wound that I hadn't realized that the wound was healing and, far from preventing my partner from bleeding out, I was in danger of causing a new bruise.

I'd fallen subconsciously into doing something many allistic partners of autistic people do. The most important thing is, as in any relationship between adults, you cannot parent your partner. You have to leave room for them to make mistakes and learn, rather than impose what you believe is best. Stubborn autists are like stubborn allistics in that way, right? Tell us we really need both of our arms, and we will have one removed to prove to you we don't.

Be prepared for your partner's diagnosis to change your relationship, possibly a lot, and to potentially keep changing it over the course of years as you both adjust. Being with someone who has just made a huge leap in understanding themself and the world around them is a trip. Everything starts coming into focus in a new light, and you have the opportunity to join them in their process of life-changing discovery. Pace yourself, get your friends on board (if your partner's okay with being out to them), and take time for yourself when you need to. You'll probably be doing a lot of renegotiating of relationship boundaries and norms, and your new relationship rules should take both your needs into account.

Your partner isn't the only one whose identity and assumptions will be shaken up. For instance, like me, you may have fallen into a caretaker or problem-solver role and, therefore, experience a bit of identity shock and realignment of priorities when your partner makes it clear that they prefer to anticipate their own needs, learn from their own mistakes, and do their equal share of the dishes—and that your behavior is inhibiting this. It seems likely that many neurotypical partners of undiagnosed autistic people have, knowingly or not, taken on other roles, like the family decision maker, the organized one, the socially adept one, the savior, the martyr, the servant . . . Some of these roles are powerfully compelling. We feel needed, like essential workers in the first months of the pandemic. But like all essential workers, we eventually become exhausted while struggling with being underpaid and under-respected.

And, let's face it, all of those roles listed above are ultimately very controlling. It can be hard to give them up. But letting these roles start to fracture presents an opportunity for both of you to question some of the baggage you've brought from childhood and past relationships and grow up together a little more. Therapy could help, and I wish I'd done it sooner—but Joe's commitment to learning and growing in emotional maturity allowed our relationship to mature as well and was a big part of what created a safe ground from which I could eventually do that work for myself.

Another pitfall I encountered that's embarrassing to remember was that I suddenly saw autism everywhere—in family members, old friends, new acquaintances' exes, some people who I knew well and others who I simply was excited to identify, probably incorrectly. I even applied this new zeal to myself. Joe brought home a copy of the initial screening assessment used in that first diagnosis. I took it, and scored just above the threshold for autism. For a few months, I was convinced that I too was autistic—I had never felt like I fit in with societal expectations and was prone to obsessions and outbursts, so it made some sense. But as I read more, I realized that I didn't really meet any of the core criteria, like having serious trouble with theory of mind, executive function, social skills, or sensory overwhelm—really, any of the criteria Joe outlines in part one. Looking back, I see that most of the boxes I checked on that test could be attributed to a heady combination of trauma, anxiety, immaturity, and a few decades of trying to put logic before empathy.[16] These things have helped me relate to and empathize with the autistic people in my life, but they don't add up to autism.

Some advice: Read a lot about autism, especially other autistic people's experiences, and try to see your partner's behaviors, body language, and habits in a new light. Everyone has different experiences and needs, so don't assume that, for example, just because some autistic YouTuber hates it when people leave the light on after leaving a room, your partner cares about that too. Instead, *ask them how they feel about various things*. See what comes up. And listen carefully. Nothing in your daily life is immune to transformation. It's very likely that you have a number of habits that will be relatively straightforward for you to change in order to make a huge difference to your partner—stuff that has kept them on the edge of overwhelm for years, but either they never realized it was valid to speak up about it or you took it personally or scoffed at them when they tried. Over the years, I've made adjustments, such as no longer putting Joe's belongings away where I think they belong ("hiding them," as Joe puts it), not cooking certain smelly foods in the house, and convening away from home when I want to get together with a group of more than six people. I know that, in turn, Joe continues to make allowances for my needs, likely many more

16 Faith here. So true from a clinical perspective. I would also add that allistics with significant trauma history find neurodivergence soothing because we often read negativity in the subtext of others, and autists have no subtext.

than I'm aware of. I *hated* learning that things I'd been doing that suited me or that I thought were a favor to Joe were actually creating sensory havoc and barriers to executive function. It was easy to react defensively at first (which, Faith adds, is a normal instinct when one's intent was lovely but the outcome was chaos). But thanks to having to talk over all these things explicitly, we're now both in the habit of speaking up and asking, and that's measurably improved our daily life and general trust.

Finally, as you learn more, it may be tempting to become the autism expert amongst your friends and family. This isn't advisable. Keep your partner's qualities that you love and respect—not autism—central to your relationship, and others will follow your lead. Remember, all autistic people are individuals who express autism in different ways.

WHAT IF YOU ONLY SUSPECT YOUR PARTNER IS AUTISTIC?

Get your facts straight, and ask how they feel about it. Maybe they've already been thinking about this too. They may dismiss this idea or react defensively. That's fine. The issue at hand is caring for their needs, not an armchair diagnosis.

How to bring it up? Faith always posits it to clients with this question: "Has anyone suggested that you may have some level of neurodivergence?" This label is far less challenging, and the question suggests that we're looking at their history and perspective rather than saying, "Hey, sis, you're clearly autistic AF!" If it's a totally new idea to them, you can offer them an article, the first part of this book, or our book *The Autism FAQ* to read and ask what they think. After they have some time to consider this, broad questions with long pauses can be helpful. We'd start with "What do you think about this? Does this sound like you?" and move into "Do you think this might be a helpful framework for you?" or "Do you think this might lead to an easier life where you could be better supported?" Again, your partner may *hate* these suggestions, because your feelings on the matter are apparent. So it's important to accept their answers, give them time to reflect on their own schedule, and keep the conversation focused on how to support their needs.

If they're open or curious, it's time to learn more. *The Autism FAQ*, Wrong Planet forums, and the #ActuallyAutistic hashtag on any social media platform are good places to start, and there are a bunch more resources out there that you can evaluate for yourself. Find a clinician, like a therapist or even a doctor, who lists autism as one of their specialties (you can search for this in the *Psychology Today* directory). Decide whether or not to pursue a formal diagnosis.

If they are completely hostile to the idea, you *have* to drop it. You are not a psychologist, and even if you are, you are too close to this situation to be objective. Maybe they'll bring it up again in their own time, maybe not. It's not appropriate for you to diagnose them or decide for them. And you might be wrong. There are a lot of conditions that can be mistaken for autism, or that go hand in hand with it, and without a diagnosis or their agreement, you can't know for sure what's up. This book can still give you advice that can help you navigate your relationship, whether or not your partner is autistic or open to the idea that they might be. You can still work on seeing and loving your partner with all their quirks, needs, and triggers and not taking these things personally. And you also don't need your partner to embrace any specific diagnosis in order to decide for yourself what you need in a relationship, communicate that clearly and specifically, and then act accordingly.

UNDERSTANDING YOUR PRIVILEGE

Joe here. Recently, on a podcast, I listened to two white women explain male privilege through the lens of the gender wage gap (white women earn 78% of what white men do for the same work, on average) and the ability to safely walk around at night. Because privilege, in this sense, refers only to a lack of barriers. And for autistic people, both of these privileges are more complicated. Worldwide, 78–89% of autistic people are unemployed. It's unsafe for autistic people to walk around at night or even during the day, because we exhibit the behaviors that police are trained to look for to deduce that someone is hiding something or being dishonest. We send up all of the red flags to law enforcement, from avoiding gaze to *too much eye contact*. We are constantly targeted because of our perceived gullibility, willingness to take people at their word, and inability to deduce the nonverbal signs of impending danger.

Once, I was standing in front of my house, waiting for a ride, when a cop claimed that a neighbor had called because of my "suspicious behavior." I asked what suspicious behavior I was exhibiting, and he said that information had not been relayed to him. He didn't understand why I was annoyed. On another occasion, I was stopped on my bicycle only because a robbery had occurred several miles behind me. For many years prior to diagnosis, I could never figure out why I was being singled out each time that I flew on an airplane, rode my bicycle past a cop, or crossed an international border. Neurodivergence comes with many difficulties in a neurophobic world, but people tend to find it especially hard to understand the ways in which it intersects with other kinds of social power structures; when I tell people the story about my neurodivergent assistant being arrested for going to the dentist, I am met with shocked stares and bewilderment because he is a white male. (For more information about interacting with law enforcement and other authorities, see chapter 5.)

Intersectionality complicates each person's relationship to privilege, and the barriers created by autism are compounded by any other barriers that a person might face due to, for example, their gender or race. This awareness can feel complicated in an interabled relationship where the neurotypical person also belongs to one or more marginalized groups. We know how easy it is to fall into the trap of thinking that only one person in a relationship can experience oppression or powerlessness, or to get caught up in Oppression Olympics, where arguments are won or lost based on who is most vulnerable to victimization. We're offering this catalog of neurotypical privilege not to encourage this type of scorekeeping, but to provide another framework through which you and your partner can understand and empathize with each other.

If your partner is (or appears to be) a cis, straight white man who's recently been diagnosed as autistic, it may be new for both of you to think about them as vulnerable; to be able to do so could make your relationship stronger than you ever imagined it could be.

Here are some realities to keep in mind in order to strengthen your relationship.

- *For an allistic, understanding what is in someone else's mind is a daily kind of psychic privilege.* To begin to understand what it's like to be autistic, spend time as an adult in a foreign culture where every custom is different from the impulse that comes naturally to you. Knowing the temper and tone of a stranger engaging with you can be the difference between safety and danger. Expecting autistic people to know what you're thinking is the same as expecting a blind person to see what's in your hand without any guidance.

- *You will likely outlive your partner.* That's just a fact. A fact we are hoping will change, but still something to be aware of. Our life expectancy is just under age 40, and, because of the social isolation resulting from how autistic people are treated, one of the leading causes of death is suicide. Autistic people face more rejection, confusion, and social isolation than most populations. Almost all of these difficulties are caused by autistic people's deep misunderstanding of social rules. As a result, autistic people are perceived as disobedient, argumentative, and deceptive. We bury this pain, may be defensive or sensitive, and end up feeling unwanted and unworthy. It takes a good decade into adulthood for all humans to develop the prefrontal cortex enough to have the critical thinking skills to refute others' criticisms. That is to say, it takes time to develop a full, adult perspective on the events in your own life.

- *The world is more dangerous for autistic people.* Autistic people have a much higher chance of suffering sexual violence or relationship abuse in our lifetimes, most likely at the hands of someone that we know. The numbers vary, but research consistently shows that 90% of autistic women and almost 70% of autistic men are sexual assault survivors, with the majority of them experiencing continual and ongoing assault. Those wounds run deep and take decades to truly get past. We also frequently experience bullying, depression, anxiety, trauma, low self-esteem, and low relationship expectations.

- *What makes sense to autistic people makes no sense to most people.* Autistic people operate based on a different kind of logic. What makes sense to us will seem highly irrational to you. Similarly, we are frequently accused of being dishonest and of committing lies of omission or paltering—the act of selectively using the truth to deceive someone. Sometimes, to avoid telling you what we don't think you want to hear, we are evasive or vague. This isn't methodical or meant to be hurtful. We are trying to accommodate your feelings—or what we understand of them. This can be resolved by talking about these instances without accusation and by approaching the conversation as an opportunity to listen as well as offering your perspective and needs. Because, let's face it, allistics tell socially acceptable lies all day long and no one calls them on it. Everything from "How are you?" to "We should hang out sometime" are polite words typically uttered without sincerity. But it's commonly accepted among allistics that your restaurant server does not want to hear how you are doing.

- *Simple actions take on new meanings for autistic people.* I learned from a young age that smiling conveys a pleasant warmth and approachability. We don't learn until later that some people use this tactic misleadingly to lure us into unsafe situations. And a bit later, we learn that some people, particularly women, are cautious of smiling strangers because they know that this can signal danger or selfish motives. But still later, we learn that the warmth conveyed by a smile has an infectious quality for those we bestow it upon. We can literally make someone happier. All in all, this is a lot of power and it's mighty confusing. Is it wrong to try to make strangers feel better by smiling at them when it might make some of them uncomfortable? This is the kind of ever-present question that keeps autistics up at night.

- *You can probably handle a lot more sensory input than we can.* Going to the grocery store may be a completely overwhelming experience for us. The lights, the sounds, the smells, the crowds, the requirements to figure out what to buy (and which version), to stay on budget, to navigate various interpersonal interactions, to not drop a glass jar of spaghetti sauce in the middle of aisle nine—it's a lot. And if it's just a slightly tedious Saturday morning errand for you, it might take a lot for you to notice the effect it has on us. Experiencing the world through the senses of an autistic person, mundane activities become almost impossible: think about riding the bus, going to a party or bar, putting on uncomfortable clothes to spend the day in an office with an open floor plan and buzzing fluorescent lights, going to a crowded beach under the cruel rays of the sun. We can probably do some or all of these things, but doing them all the time is going to take a lot out of us and not leave us a ton of bandwidth for what's important to us, including our relationships.

ACCEPTANCE

There is no way around it: autistic people are not treated the same way as allistic people. Even if an autistic person were to say the same authentic phrase as an allistic person, with perfect theatrical performance, they would be met with annoyance, confusion, or fear instead of understanding or empathy. This is because autistic people lack that "special sauce" that breeds relationships. People just don't know what to make of them. If you don't understand what this means, ask your loved one and pay attention to the social dynamics they experience. For example, if I (Joe) leave the house, it is invariable that at least one person regards me as if I have visible leprosy. It's like everyone is staring at us, thinking, "There is something wrong with you, and I don't want to stick around long enough to find out what it is." Brains are hardwired for protection, meaning we will err on the side of fear. So anyone who isn't aware of how autists move through the world sees me as sus.

Trying to cope with all of this, almost every autistic person has stories of running away, wandering the earth seeking a group to belong to, innumerable failed relationships and marriages, assaults and other forms of victimization due to our gullibility and vulnerability, arrests, losing child custody, and failed efforts at education and employment. I really thought my failures and the way that I had been treated because of my neurodivergent behaviors were uniquely horrifying until I met other autistic people, each of whom had variations on the same stories. Although I don't wish this pain on any human, it helped to not feel so alone. And dark as they may be, these failures are learning experiences on the way to achieving our meaning and purpose.

The need for acceptance is the biggest reason that believing autistic people is so important. Trusting and believing in the lived experience of all autistic people is the most healing thing you can do. Every autistic person has stories and experiences of having their personhood cut down or of being told that things didn't happen the way that they remember. Weekly, if not daily, others tell autistic people that they are "wrong" or simply deny their autism. Ask your partner about some of these stories. Listen and validate their experiences every day.

The big thing to understand about your autistic partner is that knowing they are autistic doesn't change who they are—but it may change how they see themself, their relationships, and their role in the world. And it might change your perspective on them and how you both understand your relationship. But it's also really important to remember that not everything about your partner, or about your relationship, can be explained by autism. Don't put that burden on them. They are also an individual with a complex personality shaped by many experiences, interests, and values. Autism is more like the lens through which they experience their life and—more importantly—is usually a major factor in how others view and treat them. Still, it's not the summation of their personhood.

Most of the time, when you hear talk about autism from advocacy organizations, it's regarding "autism awareness." It was a well-intended approach: the neurotypical brain engages with "disabled people" by offering pity. Rather than seeing autistic people as equals who face different challenges and express themselves in unfamiliar ways, "awareness" became another way to regard autistic people as something to keep at arm's length, similarly to how poor people are regarded in capitalist society. Fundamentally, this is why autistic people need acceptance, equity, and inclusion—not just awareness.

Typically, a marginal group is offered a seat at the table when it can act like the dominant majority. Gay rights groups were told the same thing in the 1970s: that they would be accepted when they behaved like straight people. Women are rewarded for mimicking the toxic behaviors perpetuated by the patriarchy. A more helpful approach is to meet your partner where they are and accept them for how they are, as long as that relationship isn't toxic for you.

For over 700 years, the town of Geel, Belgium, has had a saying: "Half of Geel is crazy, and the rest is half crazy." Based on the legend of Dymphna, the Catholic patron saint of the mentally ill (who was also the decapitated victim of her mentally ill father), the town made it a social responsibility to care for the mental health of all of its citizens. There's a long-standing tradition in Geel of taking in mentally ill strangers to live in your home. Through this care, nobody is trying to "change" or "fix" people. One family recalls taking in a man who hallucinated lions; rather than denying that the lions were real, the family would protect the man from these lions until they no longer appeared in his visions. Through acceptance and creating bonds with strangers, where there is no emotional baggage or negative past experience, even the most extreme cases improve. This is an excellent example of the kind of acceptance that autistic people need.

In *The World According to Mister Rogers*, Fred Rogers reframed ability straightforwardly:

> Part of the problem with the word "disabilities" is that it immediately suggests an inability to see or hear or walk or do other things that many of us take for granted. But what of people who can't feel? Or talk about their feelings? Or manage their feelings in constructive ways? What of people who aren't able to form close and strong relationships? And people who cannot find fulfillment in their lives, or those who have lost hope, who live in disappointment and bitterness and find in life no joy, no love? These, it seems to me, are the real disabilities.

This profoundly drove me (Joe) to tears because it felt like Mr. Rogers was singularly describing me. It felt like he understood what I was going through in a way that no one else ever seemed to. He understood the pain, the fear, the loneliness, and the results of these feelings. I wondered if things might be different if I lived in Geel.

Even if we don't know that we are autistic, we know that we are different from others. We know the truth of our lived experiences. The repeated experience of *not being heard, understood, or believed* is what creates our co-occurring symptoms. Autism, in and of itself, is not a disability. Neurodivergence isn't a cute word we are using to hide the truth—it's the most accurate term we have for explicating the truth. Which means that living as an autistic person in a neuronormative world full of triggering encounters and sensory overload is what creates the disability. The constant denial of our inner lives is what causes depression, isolation, guilt, anxiety, migraines, agoraphobia, sleeplessness, weight loss or gain, weakened immune system, anger, confusion, and trauma. We are constantly being gaslit, told that what we experience isn't the "truth." If people were respectful, loving, and honoring of what our perceptions and lives are like, we wouldn't have the problems that we do. This is why awareness and acceptance are so important to us living healthy, whole, happy, self-sufficient lives.

For many interabled relationships, the biggest misstep is to assume that the relationship's "solution" is to "train" the autistic person into normative allistic behaviors. This is essentially what ABA therapy does to autistic children. It's an attempt to torture the autism out by punishing expressions of autism and rewarding neuronormative behavior. Sure, you can find autistics who feel that they benefited from ABA therapy, and it isn't our place to judge someone else's experiences. But the vast majority of people we have talked to found that it broke their spirit and disconnected them from their true selves. Imagine if we tried to retrain allistics to have the strengths and abilities of an autistic person! Do you think it would help anything? The difference is that allistics comprise the majority of the population, so their behaviors are seen as "normal." It's powerful to walk a mile in another person's shoes, but at the end of the day, we still live in our own brain.

Clearly, you love your partner, or you wouldn't be dating them *and* seeking out this reading to make your relationship better. So your role is ultimately to understand your partner's experiences and needs and accept that this is the state of your partner, rather than a phase that you can help them move past. The Gottman Method of therapy (more on this in part two!) points out that while our brains are wired to believe that we can find a more perfect partner, we are often just swapping one problem for another. By embracing the reality of your autistic partner, you can work together to form a better union.

PART TWO: BUILDING YOUR RELATIONSHIP

So that was a lot of information. Hopefully it helped you see your partner's needs and your own actions and motivations more clearly. As for how to actually improve your relationship? That's the long game. In this part of the book we'll offer you all the tools and perspectives we know that might help, and you can add those to what you already know to help you reflect on your own decisions and start conversations with your partner about how to do it better, together.

We're going to start with some relationship rules. These are not specific to autism—they're rules Faith lays down for all her couples counseling clients, because discernment requires structure. They are also incredibly helpful for relationships that are not in crisis, and since you're reading a book about how to improve your relationship, we figured these wouldn't go amiss. Here are Faith's ground rules for relational intimacy that she uses in her practice:

1) *Presume best intent (until proven otherwise).* That remark your partner made, the thing they broke, the chore they didn't do, the expression on their face, the text you saw on their phone—ask yourself what the most innocuous possible explanation is, and go with that until you know differently. Because all brains are hardwired for protection, we tend to assume that pain was delivered intentionally; most often, that is the opposite of true.

2) *You're on the same team.* It's the two of you against the problem, not the two of you against each other. Even if that problem is the result of one partner's behavior, experience, or mistake, you face it together. In that case, we are referring

back to the importance of intent and framing the situation or the action or the behavior as the problem, instead of the person.

3) *Be in your actual relationship, not its potential.* Trying to make your partner change, or waiting for them to become the person you imagine they can be, doesn't work. Imagine another 20–50 years of you both being exactly as you are. Can you accept that?

4) *Accept (and believe) accountability.* If one partner has perpetrated harm, they must take accountability for their actions. Again, this is not about intent but about impact. They must say in words that they are sorry, be ready to make any possible amends, commit to changed behavior in the future, and follow through on that commitment. And the partner who was harmed needs to believe them. If you don't or can't because of past evidence? That is something to consider in your individual counseling, because the relationship is stuck until you are able to make a decision about their apology and what it means.

5) *Show your work.* If you're doing internal work to grow, change, or be accountable, make it external. Your partner needs to know what you are working on so they can trust and support you. This goes for everything from being less critical of them to quitting smoking to trying to change careers.

6) *Communicate concretely.* All important communication between partners needs to be concrete as pavement. Use your words to express your needs, wants, and desires. This is especially important when autism is in the mix, but nobody can read minds, and you can't get what you don't

ask for. And if you detect a subtext or hidden message behind something your partner says? You need to ignore that and respond to what they actually say, and they need to do the same for you. This feels deeply scary, but after a while it is enormously freeing. I don't have to try and read minds? If they say they are fine, I am going to roll with that until/unless they say otherwise? It isn't a riddle or a puzzle? Damn, now I have time to go write the great American novel.

7) *Go to bed mad.* Seriously, no good resolution is going to happen at 3 a.m. or by saying things in anger that can't be unheard. Bedtime or not, it's always appropriate for either partner to take a break from an argument to regulate their emotions. There are a couple of subrules for this:

a) Don't use this rule to avoid the issue. The partner who calls for the break is the one responsible for reaching back out when they're ready to talk.

b) If your partner struggles with abandonment issues, make it clear that you are not leaving them, but that you need to temporarily step back from the situation in the interest of the relationship.

8) *Treat your partner like the most important person in your world.* In a struggling relationship, it's easy to start treating your partner with less consideration than you would a coworker, an acquaintance, or your barista. Take the time to remember why you fell in love with them, see the good in them, and appreciate them. This perspective shift can make all the difference.

9) *Focus on the present and future, not past behavior.* Sure, that thing your partner said eight years ago might still hurt. Do

they say things now that hurt you in similar ways? If so, deal with those issues as they come up. If not, appreciate them for having changed and grown.

10) There is no number 10. But in the interest of having a real top 10 list? Add your own personalized relationship rule here.

CHAPTER 3: GETTING ALONG

Let's face it: a lot of couples just don't get along, and their difficulties aren't more profound than that. Sometimes it is because of huge values differences that are truly irreconcilable, but more often it is the buildup of small wounds that occur when we don't communicate effectively, get reactive instead of proactive, and step on each other's traumas. Usually it's just petty stuff that pushes each other's unexamined trauma buttons.

This is where rule number one comes in. It's a lot easier to not get along and be super annoyed at your partner when you believe, however subconsciously, that they are doing whatever the annoying thing is on purpose, or worse, that they're doing it on purpose to annoy you.

In these situations, an understanding of autism can be helpful. This understanding can help you realize that, for example, your partner scowls and acts grumpy when you play music loudly while cooking not because they resent you and want to deprive you of something you like, but because they're experiencing sensory overwhelm. Or that a loud, inappropriate joke told to a group at your expense may not have been intended to make fun of or offend you (though you definitely need to address that later so they know how you felt when they said it).

Elly here. Ceasing to take things personally can also be the mechanism you need for change. When we first got together, Joe used to make a daily mention of my massive coffee habit, and brought it up to other people, too. Joe says this was intended as cute teasing or a private joke that brought us closer together. Exhibiting unusual savvy for that not-very-emotionally-intelligent period of my life, I brought it up soon after I noticed it was bothering me. When

I said that I felt self-conscious every time and not in a good way, Joe stopped immediately. It would have been just as easy to let it simmer into a long-standing resentment while expecting Joe to notice that I didn't give any positive reinforcement or maybe to read my mind. I suppose it was Joe's responsiveness to other small things that I'd said I liked or didn't like that gave me the trust that this kind of feedback would be well taken. And that modeled for me the ability to really hear it when Joe would say, "I felt X when you did Y" and change my own habits and behaviors as well.

In any relationship, it's easy to lose your connection with and thus tolerance for the other person. In a relationship with an autistic person, that's no different. If you find that you're annoyed with or embarrassed by your partner on a regular basis, that is worth investigating to find out if you need to shift your perspective, if you need to communicate differently, or if you just don't like them very much and need to stop tormenting both of you by staying in the relationship. I had a moment of clarity when we went to England together and Joe took to speaking loudly in a fake British accent while walking down the street, in public, surrounded by actual British people. This was absolutely mortifying, but I was delighted to realize that it was the first time I could remember ever being embarrassed by Joe. I concluded that our relationship was in great shape and teased Joe mercilessly, and now it's one of our many running jokes.

But what if I was actually embarrassed by Joe all the time? If I stayed in the relationship and didn't address it, that would be pretty apocalyptic in one of four ways, which Faith will explain here:

John and Julie Gottman are relationship researchers and real-life married-to-each-other people. They have spent decades researching what ends relationships and what keeps them thriving and found that many, many, many times it comes down to four behaviors that the good Drs. Gottman have termed the four horsemen (yes, absolutely a nod to the Christian scriptures delineating the end of the world): criticism, contempt, defensiveness, and stonewalling. And before you spiral into an "oh shit, it me" moment, know that we all struggle with these behaviors. Life is hard, we all have baggage, and we all are looking for ways to protect ourselves from pain. But working on these behaviors doesn't just make us better and kinder partners; it is also incredibly helpful for our own headspace. Otherwise we are living in an emotional soup of sad and angry all the time.

So let's talk about what these terms mean for your relationship with your autistic partner.

- **Criticism:** Okay, your partner did something shitty, annoying, or not in the way you would have done it. Because even though they are autistic, they still aren't perfect. When we fall out of sync with our partner it can be really easy to pick at every little thing they do, firing off a barrage of criticisms about things that may not matter very much in the big picture but that get on your nerves in the moment. It can also be tempting to use constant criticisms as a way to try to obliquely communicate your own needs or discomfort. If they really mess up, the temptation is to bring up their giant mistake every time you're upset at them for something else, or to generalize it into a personality flaw, which leads us to . . .

- **Contempt:** Contempt for another person is pretty fucked up. Contempt happens when we conflate behavior with personhood and evaluate someone as worthless and unwanted because of their behavior. Remember a time when you felt truly misunderstood, when you were ridiculed and mocked as you were trying to do your best. You were treated with contempt instead of support and understanding. Of all of these horsemen, contempt is the biggest predictor of relationship breakup. Autistic people are treated with contempt every day and really don't need more of it at home.

- *Defensiveness:* This is a common response to uncomfortable feedback. We don't like taking it on the chin when we fuck up, and it feels like an attack on our personhood instead of a conversation about our behavior. Whether the feedback we are getting is accurate or unjust, listening to what is being communicated in order to understand/problem solve/take accountability is vital to a healthy relationship. It is very easy to take things your autistic partner says personally when they're simply stating a fact without a greater agenda, and training yourself out of this reaction can be a long road.

- *Stonewalling:* This is where we shut down and disengage. The Drs. Gottman point out that it usually happens in response to expressed contempt. We have talked a lot in this book about becoming physiologically flooded and the need to take breaks. Sometimes for autistic people those breaks may be extra long and the shutdowns may be extra intense. But the goal of these breaks is to self-regulate and then come back to the conversation; stonewalling, on the other hand, is continuous shutdown and disengagement, making it nearly impossible to have a discussion or argument about something important to the relationship.

Now, since we are here to offer solutions, not just to discuss problems, let's also cover what the Gottmans refer to as the antidotes to the four horsemen.

- *Instead of criticism, try gentle start-up:* Feedback and criticism are two different things. Remember the Dr. Faith rule of presuming best intent? Still applies. Criticism says, "I can't believe you did that! You are so selfish and mean!" Feedback says, "My feelings were hurt when you did XYZ. I was scared and I didn't like what was happening . . . can we talk about a different way to handle those kinds of situations?" To give effective feedback, communicate with "I" statements. Instead of jumping in with what your partner did wrong, focus on the emotional impact for you and what positive behavior you are requesting instead. If your partner was supposed to pick up eggs on the way home and forgot, criticism could sound like "You don't care about me enough to prioritize my requests!" By contrast, gentle start-up would sound like "I was really frustrated when you forgot to pick up eggs on your way home; I had been counting on them to cook dinner for us. Could you please run out and get them now, and can we figure out a reminder system, like a note in your phone, to help you remember in the future?"

- *Instead of contempt, try building a culture of appreciation:* Every human being is an enormous pain in the ass. I'd like to say that excludes all of us . . . because you are reading our book, so you are clearly good people. But alas, you (and we) are still obnoxious just because we're all flawed, evolving, imperfect creatures. If we focus on those flaws and struggles and frustrations, we end up becoming increasingly unhappy with our partners and our relationship with them. The Gottmans encourage focusing on the qualities you like about your partner and building positive interactions with them as a buffer against frustration turning into contempt.

Back to the same forgetful partner: take a moment to tell them (and remind yourself) that, for example, you admire their skill and focus at driving and always feel safer knowing that they'll never be checking their messages or to-do lists as they cruise to a stoplight . . . even if it means the errand you asked for might slip their mind.

- *Instead of defensiveness, try taking responsibility:* Defensiveness is when we avoid taking blame. If our behavior is called out as harmful, we are often taken by surprise and get upset because we didn't intend harm. Taking responsibility (shared) for the exchange or accountability (individual) if it's all on you breaks the fight cycle. Maybe it turns out that you bear some of the responsibility for the forgotten errand: "The whole reason I asked you to get those eggs today is that I spaced and left them off my big weekly shopping list on Saturday morning, so it's not fair of me to be so upset with you for not picking up my slack."

- *Instead of stonewalling, try physiological self-soothing:* Stonewalling happens when we become overwhelmed and disengaged, right? This is why I maintain that it's fine to go to bed angry. The Gottmans did an interesting experiment where they filmed fighting couples. After 15 minutes, they would stop the couple, claiming that they had to change the microphones around. They would then ask the couple to go hang out and read a magazine and chill for like half an hour. And? You guessed it. After a half-hour break, couples came back calmer and more effective in their communication strategies. Maybe instead of losing it at your honey over forgetting the eggs, you take a head-clearing walk . . . to the convenience store.

Like with any other marginality or disability, it's also so important to remember that your autistic partner is vulnerable in some ways you might not relate to. In addition to likely being completely ineffective at communicating any message to your literal-minded autistic partner, your use of any of the horsemen tactics in your relationship also has the potential to do extra harm to them. This is an important consideration whenever you reach an impasse or have a conflict in your relationship, and it's possible that making accommodations that feel unequal in the moment could actually solve all your problems. If you need to break up because you just don't like your partner anymore or are sick of them not seeming to pull their weight in the relationship, do it. But if you're not at that point, think about what extra efforts you might be able to make to create conditions where you can enjoy each other's company as equals. Consider how, if your partner was in a wheelchair, you wouldn't store things that they needed every day on a high shelf, or yell at them for not putting stuff back up there. Likewise, there are accommodations you can make for your autistic partner by considering their individual needs—including literal ones we'll discuss in the housekeeping section in chapter 4. It might be easy to interpret your autistic partner's behaviors as lazy, messy, not caring, not respecting you, etc., but that interpretation is usually incorrect. If you are having trouble connecting, getting along, or even liking each other, remember that your partner's marginality means it's extra easy for anyone around them to unwittingly use these horsemen tactics to be a bully. Don't be that bully.

BASIC TRUST, RESPECT, AND LOGISTICS

Joe here. Elly and I have a very amusing problem when we are getting ready to go somewhere together but don't have a particular timeline. We will both gradually get ready and then each wait for the other to ask the "Are you ready to go?" question, thinking that we are politely accommodating the other's needs. It happens about once per week that one of us is packing a bag and the other is in another room, reading a book. We are both ready to walk out the door but think that the other person is not. Sometimes this process can take up to an hour before someone thinks to say something. She is accommodating around this issue, understanding that sometimes I am really chugging along on something important to me, and doesn't put sole fault on either of us. If you find yourself in this situation, she suggests clarifying verbally with "I am ready to go, and I'm going to read while I wait for you."

When you are ready to go out the door and your partner is not, it can feel like they aren't respecting you or even listening. This is a microcosm of social needs in interabled relationships. Here are some tips to help you understand and accommodate your partner's needs while also communicating your own.

- *Your partner needs a reason to get out of bed every day.* The key life-preserving function for autistic people is connecting our special interests to our meaning and passion and translating those interests into actionable activities. For some people that's video games. For Joe, it's book publishing. For others it's reading about dinosaurs or obsessing over clothing fibers. Kenny Shopsin, a chef and a New York institution, talked about how all people need *arbitrary stupid goals*. This doesn't mean they are literally arbitrary and stupid, but it is still fine if they are. Because it doesn't matter either way. Goals give you things to look forward to, and the real meat of life happens during the pursuit of these goals. Your partner has probably been shamed for this interest many times in their life, so these activities require your regular verbal validation, respect, and support. Look at it this way:

by allowing your partner to focus on their meaning and purpose, you are giving them time with their reason to live.

- *Balance the teeter-totter between your needs.* Even when you understand the importance of your partner's needs, it's still annoying when your partner is focused on their meaning and purpose when you want to go out the door. You'll still want to hold on to that firm boundary of "If you aren't ready in 20 minutes, I'm going without you." You can explain that you made a commitment to be somewhere or you just really want to go. While it might sound heartless in the context of what's going on, it's clear and actionable. It affords you self-respect and allows your partner the agency to make a decision instead of being punished.

- *Give your partner time alone.* To manage their cognitive load, autistic people need to match the amount of time they spend around other people with an equal amount of time to unwind. So if your partner spends eight hours at a job where they have to talk to other people, they will be irritable if they don't also have eight hours of alone time. (Joe here: I have found that my body will actually decide to sleep less in order to ensure that I have a sufficient amount of time to unwind in private every day.)

- *Listen to your partner unload but don't be a pushover.* When autistic people spend time apart from their partners, they compound thoughts, ideas, and feelings all day. When your partner sees you at the end of the day, they will likely explode into an unexpected monologue. Remember that for autistic people, communication is information exchange *only*—not emotional relating. If you want to emotionally relate with your partner, listen to them talk about their day, engage with some of what was exciting, stimulating, and difficult, and then talk about your own day. If there is an ongoing problem where this exchange is not mutual, insist that they listen to you tell them about your day after telling you about theirs.

• *Help your partner make sense of things.* When autistic people are inundated with too much information, it's hard for them to draw discernable, meaningful patterns from it. This is an area where you can help clarify and interpret. For instance, if your partner is clearly overwhelmed by the menu board at a crowded takeout counter, you can point out something that they've enjoyed in the past, offer to narrow down their choices, or even offer to order for them. If you're both in a conversation with someone else at a noisy party, you can help your partner follow the conversation by restating the other person's words within your own responses. ("What are we doing next weekend? Oh, we're planning to clean out the basement.") If your partner is stymied by an email from an indirect communicator or government agency, you can offer to try to interpret. Don't be their parent, though. This type of support is appropriate to offer, but do ask first, or at the very least ask later if what you did was helpful and if and when you should do it again. And make sure they have the opportunity to similarly support you in turn if you are overwhelmed in an area where they've mastered the formula.

• *Understand that your partner's emotional actions are not intended as cold.* You may be frustrated when your partner seems a little mechanical on, say, Valentine's Day. You may feel sidelined by the actions they are performing to achieve their goal, even if that goal is to give you a present or make you feel loved. If you tell them to get you flowers, they most likely will, but you probably really want more than that. The interaction may feel scripted, and you may feel interchangeable with someone else. This is probably because your partner is struggling with the emotional aspects of the communication, well-meaning as they may be. The good news is that if you can engage with this as a problem you're facing together (rule two!), it is solvable. Make sure to point it out whenever your partner does something that leads to you feeling especially loved and appreciated. Don't be condescending or snarky about it: "I feel really loved when you take out the trash instead of dropping the ball and leaving it to me like you usually do" isn't going to get you anything but lifetime trash duty. Just choose a quiet moment to say how you feel. Try something more like, "I felt so cared for when you offered to pick me up from the airport." Or show appreciation in the moment with something like, "You brought me coffee? You are officially way hotter than Paul Rudd!"

- *Praise your date honestly for their best qualities.* Give them a gradual push towards *their* goals and meaning and purpose. Routinely single out and verbalize the things that you respect most about them. Talk about their accomplishments publicly and with genuine zeal. Other people will notice this and it will affect how they see your partner. It will push the envelope of what others think of as "normal" and "acceptable."

- *Teach and inspire each other instead of setting yourself up as the expert or boss.* You can still help your partner, with their consent, just as they can help you with things they're better at. Lessons can be imparted nonverbally, taught through actions, or learned through immersion. Joe taught me (Elly) to make a budget, organize my finances to make my taxes easier, and have difficult conversations with people who haven't kept their commitments. When I asked about what Joe's learned from me, the response was, "Planning snacks and meals ahead of time." I had no memory of passing on any such skill, so Joe elaborated: "You didn't tell me how to, it's more that you modeled it. That's a much better way to learn, and not condescending. Before I knew you, my meals were impulsive, so if I didn't plan, I wouldn't always eat." And it's true; I can't put my finger on exactly when it happened, but at some point I stopped worrying that Joe wouldn't eat if I didn't magically appear with a granola bar. It must have been around the same time that I was hovering with an offer of food and Joe said in an exasperated tone, "It's not your responsibility to make sure that I eat. That's my job."

• *Talk to your partner to draw out their specific needs and share yours.* What black-and-white thinking governs their world? Can the various items on their plate be touching? What happens if they accidentally touch? Should you fix it without them noticing or take that plate for yourself? And don't forget to communicate your needs as well. If you need your partner to have a conversation with you for 20 minutes each day when you get home from work, state that clearly and specifically. If you can't date someone who gets drunk every day, it's important to communicate that clearly to your partner. Be clear that it is their choice, whereas your boundary is about how this issue affects you. You aren't saying they aren't allowed to drink like that; you are saying that if it's a problem for you and isn't for them, you may need to change the nature of your relationship.

More importantly, learn to laugh together when black-and-white thinking creates comedic scenarios. For example, Joe once told a therapist that it's wrong for guitar players to sit down during a performance. Troubled by this, the therapist brought it up during several more sessions, trying to argue the point that a guitar player *can* sit while performing and explaining that her husband is one such performer. Today, Joe can realize that this idea was a product of growing up in the world of punk rock and that these rules don't necessarily apply to all genres of music. It's funny that this rule felt so disruptive in therapy.

- *Accept your partner's needs even when they don't make sense to you.* Joe here. Sometimes something completely unexpected can set your partner off. For autistic people, there are "right" and "wrong" ways of doing things (see the example about the guitar player above). These internal systems of right and wrong are mostly overt efforts to create a predictable environment and control what stimulus gets into our brains. To the untrained allistic, it appears controlling, and we can be pretty intense about things like how many guests can be in our home at once, slightly changed plans, or where we sit on the couch. We also tend to be picky eaters, as discussed in chapter 1. If something is over- or undercooked, it's nauseating to us because it's "wrong." Sometimes we need absolute silence to eat. When you're put out by some odd-seeming need, demand, or behavior, the worst thing you can do is bring the story to your allistic friends to seek validation that your partner is a giant weirdo and therefore not worth taking seriously. Instead, whatever your partner's need is, take them at their word. Talk it out and make mutual accommodations and adjustments until you find something that works for you both. Your partner's particularities shouldn't prevent you from sitting down to play guitar any time you want or need to, but you *can* accommodate them by not taking it personally if they choose to listen to your seated performance while facing another direction.

CONNECTION

Autistic people relate differently than allistics do. Neither way is "correct." When you try to relate with your partner emotionally to understand their inner story, they will often seem closed off because they aren't sharing in the way that you hoped for or expected. Autistic people can seem "standoffish" when they simply have no information to impart at that time. Accessing their own emotions is very difficult at times, and it's also difficult to verbalize and disclose their inner thoughts and feelings. Even remembering who they are at their core is a struggle most of the time and requires intense time and effort. Fortunately, this is not a permanent state. It's resolvable.

In a relationship, the emotional distance between people tends to fluctuate over time. When the emotional distance in your relationship increases for the first time, it can feel uncomfortable or like the relationship is crumbling, but often it's just a natural shift as everyone becomes more comfortable and feels that they can focus on a different aspect of their life, knowing their relationship is on solid ground. For most autistic people, the most comfortable social relationship is like that between a cat and a person, where the two parties perform unrelated activities in proximity to each other. When kids do it we call it *parallel play*, which is an apt descriptor.

What is the adult version of parallel play? It's the ability to spend quality time together without doing the same thing. Maybe one person reads while the other assembles a puzzle, or two people each do their own homework silently. Maybe you're watching TV together snuggled up side by side, but you have different shows playing on your separate devices. A cornerstone of Joe and Elly's relationship is for one person to play records while the other cooks dinner. Activities like cooking dinner together, which might feel equitable or cozy in a non-mixed relationship, can feel uncomfortable for either partner in an interabled relationship. The autistic partner will have *very strong* ideas and preferences for what goes in the stir fry and how the broccoli is chopped, which can challenge expectations for both partners. For example, early on in their relationship, Joe and Elly realized that they had grown up with very different versions of pizza. Of course, Elly grew up in the town where pizza was invented, so Joe bowed to her authenticity and was willing to try the other kind. This made them closer, but in many cases, the sort of activities that partners share in a relationship may feel strained or give you the sense that you're missing each other.[17]

There may be other times when you commit to the relationship and get comfortable, but to your partner it feels like the threads holding it together are wearing out. It's important to understand your partner's tendencies to lean in and out of the relationship. In the beginning, the autistic partner will call too much and overstay their welcome. Then they will gradually withdraw as they settle into the relationship and may appear passive and disconnected.[18]

17 Faith here, just to point out that takeout exists . . . one of you can get amazing New York–style pizza and the other partner can get wrong pizza and everyone is happy and has lots of leftovers for breakfast.

18 If you're familiar with attachment theory, you may think that your autistic partner is avoidant. While research has demonstrated that avoidant attachment is more common among autists, there isn't any research that demonstrates whether their attachment style is mediated by a trauma history or is a product of executive functioning differences. Since anxious attachment levels are the same among autists and allistics, it's a good guess that the avoidance is a trauma response, not a neurodivergence response.

This withdrawal may be related to the fact that many autistic people have a false certitude (informed by trauma) that they are going to be dumped, or that all good things must end and they have no agency in their lives. After a sufficient number of prior failures in life, a person begins to feel doomed to this lack of agency, which results in maladaptive decision making and an inevitable deterioration. If the autistic partner becomes bored and withdraws, the allistic partner should wait and give similar space. It's a way of giving space that often feels counterintuitive. Try to use this withdrawal as an opportunity to talk with yourself about the inner story and feelings of the partner. Then try to engage about these points later, while listening more than talking. They may not be ready to have that conversation yet or may not understand their own feelings or actions. Similarly, use this time to think about your own needs and feelings and how best to get them met. Script out ways to have these conversations.

Logically, it may seem like two people simultaneously withdrawing from a relationship will cause it to end; but, in fact, these interactions will show your partner that you can give them space when they need it without ending the relationship and that you can talk about these things when they are ready. The space can also pique the interest of the autistic partner and cause them to engage in the relationship again. This doesn't mean you have to push aside your own needs on their behalf, and these dynamics should be discussed. Autistic people are oblivious to the concept of emotional reciprocity that most relationships thrive on until they can intellectually understand it. Helping your partner to see what a healthy give-and-take looks like will empower them to see their own agency in your relationship.

Want a quick tip to feel closer on a daily basis? Stop asking open-ended questions like "How are you?" or "How was work/school/the event/your day?" Try something more specific and thoughtful, like "What did your boss have to say about the report?" or "What were the best and worst parts of the trip?" or "Did you learn anything new?" You are likely to receive more thoughtful, complete answers that are much more rewarding and revealing about the inner world of your partner.

Another key area of connection is physical touch. For many people, the presence or absence of that is what indicates the health of our connection much more than any other factor. We'll get into sex later, but there is so much more potential physical connection throughout every day. It's possible that either you or your partner are just tolerating the other's way of showing physical affection.

Elly here. In our first week of dating, I initiated a kiss with Joe while standing on a street corner. Joe reciprocated, then after it ended said, "I can't usually do that." I assumed that Joe had hang-ups about public displays of affection. When I finally asked about it, years later, it turned out Joe was concerned about falling over. Either way, I cut it out with the public kissing, but it would have been smarter to ask right away—or even better, ask first. Your autistic partner might not like to hug or kiss or be lightly touched on the small of their back as you pass each other in the kitchen, or they might only enjoy these things under specific circumstances, and you'll never know unless you ask.

Connecting over interests is another key area that can be challenging when one person's interests are all-consuming for them. Of course, you might be lucky enough that you are both deeply interested in things with enough overlap that you'll always have equal expertise to draw on while still being able to share something new with your partner. But it's not uncommon to find that your autistic partner's capacity to talk about their area of deep interest far exceeds your capacity to listen, and it can be all too easy to get into the habit of tuning them out, just nodding and smiling and thinking your own thoughts while they speak. This isn't great for you, them, or your relationship, so instead figure out your boundaries at that moment and state them out loud. If you have the whole morning ahead of you, and you'd like to hear your partner's update about the podcast they just listened to, then give them your full attention, ask clarifying questions, and be a full participant. But if they launch into a story or explanation an hour before you go to bed and you have stuff you need to do, let your partner know, "I have 10 minutes right now, can you just give me the quick summary and tell me the details on Saturday?" Or even "I'm so sorry but I don't think I can be a good listener right now, can we put a pin in it while we figure out how we're handling tomorrow's schedule?"

The best way to maintain interest, though, is to learn about their area of interest yourself so you can be an informed conversationalist. Joe has an encyclopedic knowledge of and abiding passion for '90s Bay Area punk music that I (Elly) will never match, but I've gotten to really like a few of the bands that I've learned about, and we can enjoy listening to records together and discussing them from our different perspectives. Joe has a lot of stories about a particular dynamic within a band or at a label, and it's fun to dissect these stories, critically examine the various factors at play, and relate them to other experiences we've had.

By the way, it is also perfectly acceptable to tell your partner that they've already told you something, or that you already have a certain level of knowledge. Autistic people have trouble knowing what other people already know, and anyone who's super excited about a topic may not remember that they've already told you that story six times. If you remind them kindly of how up to speed you are, they may appreciate the assist.[19]

---

19 Faith here. Whether neurodivergent or not, we all repeat ourselves (therapists

COMMUNICATION

Joe here. Before my diagnosis, I went out to dinner with the founder of a company that my then wife and I were doing business with. As the check was dropped off, my wife stepped on my flip-flopped foot repeatedly with increasing force. Perplexed, I asked her to please stop stepping on my foot. She grew angry with me. After we left, she said that she was trying to tell me to pay the whole bill since the other party had paid for it last time. I asked why she didn't just say that clearly so that I could understand. She stormed off in disgust.

This exchange summarizes our relationship and explains how frustrating and confusing most communication is for both parties in neurologically mixed relationships. To minimize these frustrations, it's worth approaching communication as though there is a language barrier. Words and phrases may mean very different things to each of you, and it may take a couple of years for you to truly be able to understand each other most of the time. Faith likes to talk about the four levels of communication, a concept she learned from neuro-linguistic programming. When any two people's communication breaks down, it usually happens on one of the following levels:

1) **What you mean to say isn't fully executed or thought out.**
   Elly is a repeat offender at intending to ask a question, but actually making a statement and then waiting for Joe to verify or correct it. All Joe hears is Elly making a (likely incorrect) statement. This is probably the source of a solid 30% of all conflict in the relationship.

---

are the worst at it because we have trained ourselves into repeating things several times in several ways so they will eventually filter into a client who is overwhelmed and isn't catching everything you're saying . . . apologies on behalf of all of us). I try to say something akin to "Oh yes, I remember you telling me about that! I love that so much!" Or "That was so awful, my heart still hurts for you" or whatever recognition/feedback is appropriate. You are telling them you remember, but in a way that doesn't make you seem annoyed by the story.

2) **What actually comes out of your mouth does not reflect what you mean.** Maybe you are thinking "I am hurt and frustrated" and what comes out is "Why are you such an asshole?" Or maybe you just misspoke; you think you said "Dan" but you actually said "David" and confusion reigns.

3) **What they actually hear is not what you said.** We all have a tendency to only half-listen and make assumptions about where our partner is going with a sentence. So we check out and miss where they were *actually* going with the sentence.

4) **They think you mean something other than what you said.** Have you ever had or been present for one of those horrible arguments where one person says, "What do you want for dinner? I'm good with whatever," and the other person ties themself up in knots trying to figure out what their partner *really* wants rather than just believing them? Yup, that's what we're talking about here. Usually this is the autistic partner saying what they mean and the allistic partner attempting to locate a hidden meaning.

Allistic communication norms, especially for indirect communicators, tend to cause confusion on all of these levels. It is inherently taxing on an autistic's energy to interact with an allistic, because allistics' language is coded and what they actually say is often very different from what they mean. "Have you taken out the trash yet?" is *pressure*, but phrased as a *request for information*. Instead, phrase it as a clear request, such as "Can you please take out the trash before you go to bed?" Instead of saying, "There's a rack right there that you could hang your coat on"—the snark of which is likely to be lost on your autistic partner, who will wonder why you're reciting an irrelevant fact to them—try, "Would you please always hang up your coat on the rack right after you take it off? When it is on the table or floor, it gets in my way and stresses me out." Maybe your partner has an objection to wrestling with the wobbly rack, but you can figure out how to fix it together, or they can find another place for their coat that isn't in your way. Focus on the actual reason that something is important to you and fashion that into a specific request.

Typically, only the autistic party bears the burden of translating slang, sarcasm, innuendo, contextual clues, nonverbal signals, and facial expressions to figure out what a person is intending to communicate. You can mend this fence together. If it's important for your partner to understand your meaning, state your intentions and communicate in clear and direct statements. Specific, positive feedback is tremendously helpful; this can sound like "That's the best compliment I've ever received" or "These are the best book covers that I've seen all day." It's okay if the next words out of your mouth are "But what you said earlier really hurt my feelings." Often, when the autistic partner's needs are met, they calm down, interact much better, and can accommodate your needs. Any healthy relationship is a two-way street.

It's worth noting that just because these communication barriers probably create more difficulty for the autistic partner, it's not exactly easy for the allistic partner either. As the allistic partner, you may have to work to decipher your partner's communication as well. They may deliver requests and information without the trappings that you're used to. Unless they've already learned this skill, your partner is unlikely to sit you down and say anything to the effect of "I'm going to tell you something important. [insert important thing here] Now that I've told you [important thing], what is your reaction?" They might slip that important thing in as a seeming aside or non sequitur, as you're walking out the door, or even in the middle of a sentence that initially seemed to be about something else. The key is learning to listen to and take seriously information that's delivered in a context in which you aren't expecting it.

Elly here. One thing that makes conversation with Joe never boring, but at times frustrating, is that Joe will often start a sentence with a pronoun, like "this," or just a first name, like "Jen," and my attention will then be split between listening and trying to catch up to what or who the heck this is about. Level one communication difficulty, right? Very often I will need to interrupt to say, "Which Jen?" or "Is this a continuation of what we were just talking about, or a separate topic?" Sometimes I think I know, but I've guessed wrong, leading to humorous misunderstandings. I draw on my training as a reporter to add who/what/where/when/why/how questions to our conversations to give me a structure of meaning to latch onto. And Joe is usually willing to provide this accommodation for my neurotypical brain! Similarly, Joe's doctor reports that all of her guesses about how Joe's sentences will conclude are incorrect and she's continually forced to *actually listen*. I appreciate that over the years, I've become not just a better listener, but better at processing my own thoughts and feelings so that I can communicate them in a clear and straightforward way, which has come with many benefits.

Let's look at some specific information and strategies to help bridge the communication gap for both of you.

- *Say what you mean.* Autistic people thrive with direct, clear communication. If you are acculturated to be an indirect communicator—for instance, hinting rather than saying things outright and reading between the lines of others' statements and questions—learning to code switch will be a gift to your partner and a boon to your relationship. If this is a new idea for you, looking up "ask culture vs. guess culture" is a good place to start. Think about the communication values you were brought up with and what style of communication is expected of you in the context of your culture, workplace role, class, or gender. This topic could yield some illuminating conversations with your partner and others. There is nothing inherently wrong with indirect communication, and in many situations it is a way of showing respect, but it's unlikely to be a functional way to communicate within your relationship without many years of deep understanding built up between you. It's amazing how many ingrained communication habits we carry with us that don't actually make a lot of literal sense.

- *Don't sweat the small talk.* For autistic people, communication is solely for exchanging information; it's not about sharing feelings or building connections. Since small talk doesn't communicate information of any value, the practice is terribly confusing. Your partner might not understand why this information is worth discussing. Why are you bringing up the weather, the day of the week, or some gossip? Isn't gossip bad? You can skip all that social lubrication with your autistic partner and just jump right into what you want to say, which you'll probably soon realize is better anyway.

- *Trust that your autistic partner is saying what they mean.* Another thing that is mind-blowing for allistics is that autistic people *say what they mean.* There's a scene in *The Office* when Kelly exclaims, "Darryl Philbin is the most complicated man that I've ever met. I mean, who says exactly what they're thinking? What kind of game is that?" This is your autistic partner in a nutshell. It may be hard to wrap your head around the idea that you can trust them at their word without mind games.

- *Most communication is nonverbal.* When I (Joe) went to Medellín, Colombia, my host would switch from speaking English to speaking French once I sat down, so that I could not understand. Something about my behaviors offended her, and she did not want me to be a part of the conversation. But it wouldn't have mattered anyway. 70–93% of communication is nonverbal and we are oblivious to it; humans use a different part of the brain to interpret information from faces. If you don't communicate in clear, direct, verbal language, you are literally cutting your partner out of the conversation. Would you be able to understand these sentences if you only read every seventh word? Shift your nonverbal communication to verbal communication and watch the sparks fly!

- *Even spoken language is dreadfully confusing.* Autistic people have a reputation for making inappropriate comments, often because we cannot see how what we are saying might be construed in context. For example, the sheer volume of the English language that has been given some kind of sexual connotation is ridiculous and makes innuendo hard to avoid. Perhaps when we saw someone else make the same comment, in a different context, it was to stunning applause. When you are using metaphor or a figure of speech, be mindful of whether your partner is familiar with the subtext and meaning. (See also: My current favorite visual gag is an anthropomorphic eggplant eating a hot dog.)

- *Their words will tell you more than their tone and expressions.* An autistic person may speak in a monotone, but this doesn't mean their feelings are monotonous. By the same token, they may speak in emotional tones that aren't well calibrated to what they're feeling or what the situation calls for. Many of my past partners did not understand my emotional expression and concluded that I simply did not have emotions. Elly, meanwhile, will never forget being at work one day and hearing what sounded like enraged shouting coming from another room. She ran in expecting to break up a fistfight and instead found a neurodivergent coworker describing the plot of a movie they had really enjoyed. There are still times when she'll tell me, "You seem angry, is everything okay?" and I will be confused because I was simply focusing hard on something. If you're inclined to try to read someone's mood based on their tone and body language, you may need to retrain yourself to ask rather than assuming.

- *Mind your hierarchy of information.* Why is what you are saying important? Autistic people are unable to generalize, so we focus on parts of what is being said—often not the part that you find most relevant. We tend to miss the patterns. If you want to have spaghetti for dinner, don't start by asking us what we want to do for dinner. That's an inherently dishonest way to discuss the issue. Instead, start by telling your partner what you want for dinner and then ask if that's okay with them.

- *Be specific about what you want and need.* The most common mistake that allistics make in neurologically mixed relationships is failing to express clear boundaries. Boundaries are very helpful for autistic people. "Please don't talk about my weight" or "I would like you to help me clean the house next time" are very clear. "I need help" does not necessarily mean "Can you help me carry these plants?" even if that's what you mean. And saying "Please help me carry these plants" does not necessarily mean "now" unless you say so. You must be specific and give time frames. Needing your partner to be generally more supportive is a legitimate need, but not a clear, actionable ask. Here's an example of a request that's crystal clear: "When I tell you about something I'm struggling with at work, I need you to respond right away to tell me something that I'm really good at and ask me what is going well, instead of telling me your ideas about how to solve the problem." At the same time, make sure that you leave room for your partner's perspective and specifically say that you are listening for it. They may have concerns about or barriers to fulfilling your request and may need to clear up any ambiguities about, say, the timing of what you're requesting. "Can you walk the dog this morning so I can finish organizing the taxes?" is a pretty clear request on the surface, but it doesn't include any information about *when* in the hours between midnight and 11:59 a.m. the dog needs to be walked. If that request isn't accompanied by a listening pause, I (Joe) might not have the chance to say that an appointment or a migraine might get in the way, or to counter-propose that Elly could get in the much-needed walk while I dealt with the tax documents.

- *Think about how the vast majority of every conversation is implied*. Once, I needed to pick up a prescription from my doctor. I asked what time he opened. He interpreted this as an appointment. When I showed up 15 minutes before closing, he yelled at me. I told my partner at the time, and they rolled their eyes at me, like I was an entitled idiot. I now understand that this was an autistic miscommunication. I knew that I had to get there but I didn't prioritize it as an urgent or scheduled task. I did everything else first and then wandered over there. Helping your partner understand how their actions or communication are interpreted really helps them to succeed in the long run. For example, when I made jokes about how I'd love for my partner to financially support me, I didn't understand that there were certain connotations to those statements. It wasn't enough for my partner to ask me to stop joking about this. I needed to know *why* this was inappropriate so that I could make more informed choices and better jokes in the future. Don't worry though, my jokes are top-notch today.

- *Autistic people are used to being told that our needs are secondary.* Most of our lives are about following other people's directions. You will likely need to prompt and nurture your partner into the habit of setting boundaries in order to meet their needs. They may need time alone but not know that asking for that won't scare you away. Once you have established that it's okay for them to have needs as well and that you will respect their boundaries, your partner can establish more comfort alone with you.

- *When you want a compliment, ask for it.* That's clear and easy. Your partner likes you and can find something to compliment even in times of duress. But be aware that sometimes an autistic's cognitive reactions to your moods feel inauthentic. In these moments, the motivation and care for your feelings is real even if the reaction feels programmed.

- *It helps if you talk to your partner while they do something physical.* For autistic people, having an emotional conversation is easier and more natural while walking around or doing the dishes or another task that doesn't require thinking. The other task takes away the fear and pressure—though allistic people tend to feel like we are not listening to them or not taking them seriously if we are walking in and out of the room.

- *Everything that allistics don't even notice is distracting for autistics.* Stimulus overwhelm makes it much harder for autistics to have a conversation. For example, I (Joe) routinely find that it's hard to hear someone in the presence of a bright light or cooking odors.

- *Understand how honesty works for your partner.* Something that an allistic person might consider a mistaken assumption or an exception to a rule might be perceived by an autistic person as a lie or an attack. One of the kids that I mentor was dating someone who assumed that he hadn't done something that he'd agreed to and phrased this assumption as a fact: "You didn't do that." He took this as a personal attack because he perceived himself as someone who fulfilled his commitments. And besides, he had done the thing, so in his view she was lying. Once, in my early 20s, I banged my head into a wall for an hour because I was so upset to learn that my partner smoked *sometimes* on particular occasions when they were drunk enough. I had dated a smoker in the past and found it so overwhelming and disgusting that I had a meltdown after learning that my screening question of "Do you smoke?" had yielded a half-truth. If I had known the whole truth, I wouldn't have committed to the relationship.

- *It takes a long time before autistic people can talk about feelings.* For autistic people it's always much more difficult to talk about emotions, their own or others'. When they get in a fight with someone that they care deeply about, they can get tongue tied. In general, they often find themselves incapable of forming their feelings and thoughts into words, which is called *alexithymia*. In other cases, speaking at all becomes very difficult, even for days or weeks at a time. This is called *mutism.* For you, this is probably going to be confusing and difficult as well. If your partner shuts down, it can be easy to assume they are stonewalling you, but practice empathy and don't push the issue in the moment. Withdraw to remove the pressure and bring it up again at a better time. For instance, it took Elly a couple years to realize that she shouldn't bring up any intense topic with Joe in the hour before bed, because Joe would respond monosyllabically, fall asleep in the middle of the "discussion," and remember nothing of it the next day. Now she brings up difficult topics over breakfast, while bicycling, or at times when there are other activities to divide both their focus and relieve some of the pressure.

- *Build in longer pauses.* Elly is a fast-talking East Coaster who loves an animated conversation with lots of interrupting, and Joe is a slow-talking Midwesterner given to many pauses between words, who doesn't appreciate not being able to finish a sentence. Somehow, this has not been a severe source of conflict in the relationship. Joe's pauses sometimes go on so long that Elly assumes it's the end of the thought and jumps in too soon with a response or change of subject. Is autism part of this? Maybe. A common thread for autistic people is they can take longer to think things through before speaking, processing every aspect of an idea. Elly's found it's always worthwhile to wait for Joe to fully process something and then respond, sometimes minutes later, with a fully formed, brilliantly thought-out paragraph that never would have come forth if she'd kept the conversation moving. Even though she knows the stakes, this is still just about the hardest thing in the world for her.

- *Don't underestimate an autistic person's abilities.* Joe again. A common mistake is to interpret our emotionally stunted behavior and slowed development to mean that we are stupid or incapable of understanding an intellectual point. This manifests in people talking down to us and treating us like children—behaviors that are surprisingly common. Strangers lecture me in baby talk at the airport. I'm seated in the back of restaurants, out of sight of other patrons. Someone once stopped me in my own neighborhood to suggest that I was unsafe walking around alone. When I ask probing questions to better understand something, allistics tend to repeat themselves or verbally walk around my question to redirect me to their point, like I don't understand it. To be regularly condescended to in this way lights a fuse on a relationship. We are likely to be at least as intelligent as you are, whether you can see this or not. Please respect that and you'll get more patience from us.

If you follow these guidelines you should see steady progress, however slowly. While autistic brains are wired differently, once allistic people get used to it, they often prefer interacting with autistic people and find it hard to go back to indirect communication and guessing games. It's well worth learning these skills that you and your partner can use both inside and outside of the relationship for the rest of your lives.

CONFLICT AND REPAIR

This isn't an autism-specific skill, but learning to fight well—and make up after hard things have been said—is extra important in an interabled relationship, where there may be uneven power dynamics at play. But how do you fight well? Sometimes you find yourself frustrated with your partner or in a knock-down-drag-out fight about something that you didn't even realize bothered you.

Elly and Joe here. We used to fight badly. We would hurt each other's feelings and forgive each other out of trust and affection but without necessarily having fixed the underlying problem. It was clear how far we'd come recently when we went together to meet with our tax preparer. Taxes and finances are a subject of tremendous expertise for Joe, but each time that the preparer asked questions, Elly would jump in with a very confident response before Joe could process the question. This would be great, except that Elly's answers were often incorrect, incomplete, or misleading. So afterwards we went out to a delicious lunch. Joe, somewhat unfed, brutally broached the subject with Elly, who felt a crushing feeling of failure, compounded by her own falling glucose. We had briefly reverted to roles we had held earlier in our lives.

How do you repair a conflict? Realizing that the problem felt overstated, Joe apologized, suggesting that things were fine but that perhaps Elly should not always be the first to weigh in, even if she thought that she knew the answer. But really, the biggest realization was that nothing was wrong, and the problem felt severely exaggerated because both were underfed and Joe had attempted to discuss a small problem in a way that made it feel like a massive one. Elly apologized for having taken charge of the meeting unnecessarily, and for reacting badly when Joe brought up a valid complaint. Fortunately, we have the relationship skills to listen to and hear each other, recognize each other's needs in the moment, and not double down, giving space to recognize that—instead of pointlessly squabbling with each other—if we face our foes together, we are stronger. We were already laughing about the incident within 10 minutes of our sandwiches arriving.

Here are some things to keep in mind when navigating conflicts with your partner.

- *Autistic people don't express their feelings in neurotypical ways, but they do have very intense feelings.* Conversations about conflicts can get very emotional. You may feel like you continually need to dig, prod, and pry for information, but your partner is likely trying to answer the question that they think you are asking. You may feel like they are avoiding your questions, while your partner may feel like you are asking the wrong questions to get the information that you want. These are products of the neurological differences between how autistics and allistics process narratives and experiences. To bridge this gap, be more specific and direct. Show your partner that it's okay to share, even when it may result in something that they perceive as unpleasant for you to hear. You can keep level heads by talking it out thoughtfully, respectfully, and without devaluing each other's perceptions.

- *Hurting another person is almost never an autistic person's goal.* Hurting someone requires an active theory of mind, which autistic people lack. While they are often mistaken for sociopaths, they may actually be cognitively incapable of intentionally causing hurt for its own sake. When feelings are hurt, allistics tend to experience emotional repair through apologies, talking it out, and feeling understood. Autistics, on the other hand, experience emotional repair in solitude by focusing on a special interest for hours. Sometimes engaging with a special interest or stimming is the only way to stop negative emotions. This makes it difficult for an allistic partner to see, believe, and share in the healing and to experience the conflict as resolved. You will likely need to ask specifically for what you need to have your feelings resolved. This may sound like "Can you apologize for what you said that hurt my feelings?" or "Can you give me a hug now?" It's okay to check in later to make sure neither party is actively holding resentment from that negative experience.

- *Learn to collaborate.* Remember relationship rule two: you're a team facing the problem. To work on a problem together, describe the situation clearly to your partner. Contrast the past to the present to show how ongoing conflict has worsened or improved with time. If something isn't working for one or both of you, talk about how the situation could be dealt with differently.

- *Autistic people should take responsibility for their actions, but this may not come easily.* Joe here. In these moments of conflict, it's hard for us to accept accountability because we don't feel like we did anything wrong. Rather than looking at how we hurt someone, our narrative reverts back to what we were attempting to do. It took me until my 30s to understand that there isn't a single truth; that my experience is not the same as someone else's. And slowly from there, I was able to unpack a lifetime of experiences, finally understanding why people were upset with me and how what seems to me like a series of unrelated events can create a narrative about me for others. While the appropriate response would be to listen to the issues surrounding the conflict, take responsibility for and learn from the ways that our actions affect other people unintentionally, apologize for the hurt and difficulty that we caused, and move on with our lives, the tendency of all people is to fixate on the most absurd and baseless accusations, rather than the ones that have merit. Both brain types try to paint our own innocence rather than find and own responsibility, and it can take a lot of work to move past this.

- *Honor your partner's experience as you want them to honor yours.* The fundamental difference between the two brain types is the difference between an emotional, narrative truth for an allistic and a rational, cognitive series of events for an autistic person. For the allistic, your experience is summarized by how you feel in the moment, and that truth overrides all other factors. Even if there is no evidence your brain can point to, it will access your feelings and tell you stories about your experience. This conflicts sharply with the autistic brain, which is forever seeking facts and evidence for its theses and its determinations of best practices. Autistic people prioritize objective truth above all, even above agreements or compromises. This coupled with a lifetime of trauma response tends to make allistics see autistics as argumentative, inflexible, defensive, blaming know-it-alls who can't take responsibility for their words or actions. You may be crying in your lap while your autistic partner continues doubling down on their argument. This isn't to be hurtful or difficult. They are likely honoring their truths and experience. At the same time, this isn't getting anyone what they need and it's not an acceptable way to treat someone, let alone a partner. When the situation has calmed down, talk about how their actions made you feel despite their intentions.

- *It's hard for autistic people to grasp how allistics can possibly misunderstand.* Quite a few of the autistic people that I (Joe) mentor struggle with the distinction between "intent" and "impact." One man in his 50s went as far as saying, "I don't hurt people. I help people." His self-image was such that he could not accept that he *had* hurt someone, because that wasn't how he viewed himself. I had similar problems prior to diagnosis. It's very complex for autistics to understand that we can hurt other people's feelings while trying to help them or do the "right thing." When we hurt someone, our cognitive instinct is to explain our actions, intents, and goals. To most allistics, this comes across as being argumentative or, worse, diminishing the legitimacy of their feelings. Patiently listening before sharing how you experienced your partner will help them come around to seeing how both of your experiences can be "true." If you are still having trouble convincing your partner that they hurt you, acknowledge their intentions and explain that you appreciate what their motivations were but that it didn't work out well for you. Use an innocuous example, like a time when you were running to help someone carry something but instead you scared them and they tripped. Show that both intent and impact can be true at the same time.

- *Always assume that your partner has good intentions.* That's the first rule from the beginning of this part of the book, and it's worth repeating. Even if you cannot tell by their behavior, your partner does feel deeply and feels horrible when they hurt you. They just don't know what to say or do to remedy this. Instead, they appear to shut down or act confused. They may need time alone, but you can offer some possible directions for how to remedy the situation or how to communicate what they need from you.

- *If you want to be listened to during a disagreement, listen to your partner.* They may not engage immediately or respond, but this information can be tucked away for later. If you approach solving a problem intellectually rather than emotionally or with pressure, the autistic partner will be much more receptive to engaging with it and even changing. In one couple that I (Joe) mentor, one partner was constantly lecturing the other about how he spends his money. The man knew his partner felt this way, so badgering him about it *more* wasn't going to help. I suggested that the partner stop bringing up the issue, and he changed his habits within a few months. The problem was that the pressure was creating resentment. In another example, Elly and I have long-standing differences in how we prefer to handle meals, which might seem insurmountable at first look. I prefer to eat out because I ate terrible homemade meals as a child growing up in poverty, whereas Elly doesn't like to spend so much time and money at restaurants. So we listened to each other and created a multi-faceted solution: she figured out how to cook the meals we like from restaurants at home, but *better*. And when we do go out, I pay for her food. We still eat out more than she likes and eat in more than I like, but it's a happy compromise. Your partner may argue logistics or facts at first, but it's common for us to let down our wall and agree with you unexpectedly. I have often felt steadfast in my views until I heard someone else's reasoning. Sometimes the reasoning makes no sense to me, but often I am surprised at how quickly my stance changes.

- *Change happens but it is slow.* Strong relationships are built with patience from all parties involved. Counselor and author of *Aspergirls* Rudy Simone uses the metaphor of a rock in water. The autistic partner is the rock and the allistic partner is the water. With time the rock is reshaped by the water, but first the water must conform to the rock's shape and position to begin to understand it. This requires more listening than talking—probably even more so than in most relationships. Being gentle and persistent is most helpful. With time, the allistic partner comes to understand the point of view of the autistic partner and vice versa. Compromise becomes natural for the autistic partner because they feel respected, which is a rare occurrence.

- *Practice owning your feelings.* Just because your partner's words hurt doesn't mean that your partner intended them to. More importantly, your partner can't *make* you feel a certain way. Only you can let them do that. Criticism from your partner that is hurtful is almost always intended to be helpful, even when it is thoughtless of your feelings. However, most allistics cannot deal with that and don't want the advice to begin with. If your partner gives you unwanted feedback or advice, ask for what you want instead and reward that when they give it. For example, if they tell you that your clothes don't match and you find this unhelpful, ask them to only share positive information about your appearance. They will likely interpret this as a rule in all situations, so make sure that's what you want. You may have to redirect patiently several times before they understand the specificity of what you are requesting. Your partner may also be defensive at first if they perceive that you are being surprisingly or unnecessarily harsh. But with trust and some perseverance, they should be able to hear what you are saying and understand why their words or reactions are inappropriate, and both of you should be able to get what you need.

THERAPY

If your relationship has been mired for years or decades in the types of problems described in this chapter, therapy can help immensely. You may benefit from enlisting the help of a professional to process your confusing experiences with your partner, especially if that professional is familiar with autism. I (Joe) have found therapy to be one of the most magically transformative tools for figuring out who I am and how to engage in healthy relationships. You may benefit from it, your partner would likely benefit from it, you may participate in couples counseling, or you can do all three.

However, it's important to recognize that lots of autistic people have bad experiences in therapy. This is simply because some therapists are not great at their jobs or not an appropriate match. Maybe your partner has had bad experiences with therapists trying to "fix" them. Or was subjected to behavioral specialists as a child and was told that traditional talk therapy was a waste for their "kind." This makes it even more important to find the right fit, especially if your partner is going to be involved in the therapy. You can test out therapists without committing; most will offer a free 20-minute initial conversation. If possible, have a screening session with more than one so you can increase your chances of finding someone who fits your budget, schedule, and needs and who you (and your partner, if you're pursuing couples counseling) feel comfortable talking with.

A good open-ended screener question for potential therapists is "What do you know about autism?" Therapists usually receive very little training in this realm unless they have a personal interest and have sought it out themselves, so it's important to see that they are informed, do not pathologize your partner or assume limits on their abilities, and understand the scope of the diagnosis and what it means in a relationship.

Finding a therapist who could draw from a broad pool of client knowledge was very helpful for me. This makes you feel less alone as you discover that most problems are textbook manifestations of autism, rather than just a result of you being unique or an idiot, as I was often told by many previous partners. Therapy helps us to see our behaviors in context—both the context of our lives and the context of working knowledge of the autistic brain.

Autistic people—like all people—need support, and it's best for that to come from a variety of sources, counselors among them. If *anyone* could benefit from support in navigating living in the upside down, it's autistic people. Autistic people have a clear vision to see how screwed up the world is. Therapy can help to process the resulting confusion, frustration, and urges to burn the whole thing down. A therapist who understands the unique coolness of your partner's brain can help them use the things they are best at to not just survive, but thrive.

Faith here. I receive so many referrals for neurologically mixed relationships, and I've realized that I've developed a reputation for being great at helping these partners establish better communication, boundaries, etc. But you want to know a secret? I am not doing anything that I don't do with couples where *both* partners are allistic. I am merely understanding the needs of these individuals as full people. I would say the needs are more pressing when autism is on the table, and when things don't go well it can be more distressing, but the skills are the same. For example, asking clearly and concretely for what one wants from a partner, embracing emotional accountability, taking breaks from overwhelming arguments, etc.? I encourage every couple (or throuple or any relationship configuration that comes through the door) to speak more plainly and directly, define needs and wants cleanly, and generally stop expecting someone to read your mind just because they love you.

If your partner hasn't received a proper diagnosis, talk about whether they feel that this would be beneficial to them or the relationship. A diagnosis has been tremendously beneficial to everyone that we know, but there are huge emotional stumbling blocks and waves of feelings for them to move through in order to truly process its implications.

If your partner needs to find a therapist in the midst of a crisis, you can probably help do the legwork, though keep in mind that a therapist will want to make sure that your partner wants to go to therapy and that this isn't a sneak attack. A depressed person is going to have a hard time with the executive functioning needed to find someone, make an appointment, and drag their body to said appointment—no matter their neurology. For many people over 35 especially, the stigma of therapy can be enough to keep them away because "that's for people with bigger problems." If everyone followed that logic, no one would go to therapy, ever. The reality is that everyone has real problems, both big and small.

If your partner is absolutely not willing to consider therapy, it can still be worth it for you to go for your own sake, even if you don't feel like you have a lot to unpack. For one thing, if you're in a committed relationship with someone who is struggling and won't accept help—you have things to unpack. An established therapeutic relationship will be invaluable when things do come to a point of crisis. And your therapist can help you figure out how to support your partner, or at least not stand in the way of their healing.

Suicide is a huge concern. Autistic people's suicide rates are at least two to three times that of non-autists, and the risk is compounded by other psychiatric diagnoses. This is a big part of why we're writing this book, because healthy, supportive relationships are one of the best protections out there. Either one of you being in therapy can add another layer of protection. If you aren't sure, ask your partner if they ever think about hurting or killing themself. And tell them if you ever have those thoughts. Talking about suicide directly may not come naturally, but it's one of the best ways to prevent it.

Elly and Joe here. Once, in anticipation of a difficult event where we were both worried about Joe's safety, Elly's therapist advised her about how to make a safety plan. So we did that. We created a shared document online and listed each possible outcome of the event: good, bad, or neutral. And then we listed short-, medium-, and long-term actions for each outcome. Short-term plans included the address and start time for the movie we planned to go see afterward, specific plans for what we would eat, coping skills to work through if needed, what friends we could turn to, Joe's therapist's phone number (with the therapist's advance consent to be available if needed), and the number for the county's suicide hotline in case it came to that. Medium- and long-term plans were in place to help us keep perspective. And . . . it worked. Even just having the plan helped the situation feel less overwhelming. Creating a plan for specific situations helps in the same way that scripting a conversation does. It helps you to predict the future, understand the stakes, and not be shocked by finding yourself in a sudden, difficult emotional space as the situation looms over you.

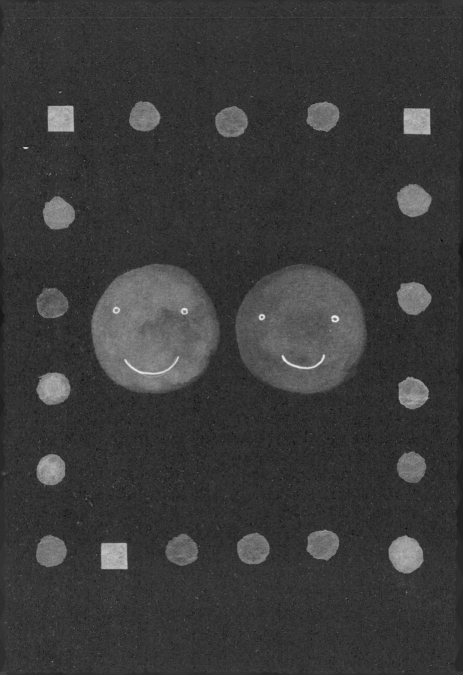

CHAPTER 4: BUILDING A LIFE TOGETHER

T(Joe) once got very upset when three of my roommates were loudly playing my records and dancing so furiously that they were making the records skip. The noise, disruption, and upset were so great that I couldn't focus on anything else. I couldn't leave the house. I was deeply incapacitated. I tried to find solace in a fourth roommate, but he said, "They are just having fun!" Why didn't anyone understand? I had one of the most embarrassing public meltdowns of my adult life, screaming, crying, and pleading in front of everyone that I lived with, who each summarily dismissed my feelings as ridiculous. It was the sort of thing that people picture when they hear the word "autistic." This experience was many years before my diagnosis, and I suspect my autistic nature is what led me into this living situation to begin with. I assumed that I'd forever live with 10 roommates and be deeply upset. But as we age, we learn how to better get a handle on things.

Elly here. Reading this, I recall how 10 years ago, our record player was in the living room and every time I walked across the floor, the record would skip and Joe would snap at me. I never understood until now why that upset Joe so much. We finally moved the stereo cabinet onto a level part of the floor in a different room, and the problem was solved. It was simple. There was no disagreement, just a stated problem and a simple solution—even if I didn't share or even understand the need for it. Because you don't have perfect transparency on what your partner is thinking or feeling, and they may have trust issues around this stuff, it's important to ask them how you can support them.

Below, Joe has laid out some basic guidelines you can follow to begin working towards building a harmonious life together.

- *Good ground rules make everyone much happier.* An autistic person's home should be their sanctuary. Giving requested space and negotiating sufficient time alone will produce greater harmony and team building. (But we'll still maintain our tendency to steal the covers.) Once a rule is agreed on, stick to it whenever possible and talk about it if you need to vary. This also applies to unspoken rules and commitments: If you consistently behave a certain way, like taking a break from work to eat lunch together at 1 p.m. every day, we may feel confused or betrayed if you start skipping days, even if there never was a "lunch is always at 1 p.m." conversation.

- *Help your partner maintain focus.* Autistic people shut out aspects of our environment so we are not overwhelmed by them. As a result, we tend to get lost, miss our turns, and otherwise appear foolish. Redirecting your partner to which aspects of the environment are relevant to the task at hand goes a long way. For example, in a crowded room, autistic people tend to get overwhelmed by the lack of clear task structure. Reminding your partner why you are there and offering some specific tasks, such as "Talk to Linda to see if that job is still available" or "Remember to ask if they still want to get together and talk shop," can really help. So can simply refraining from chatting with your partner while they are focused on something. When I have headphones on, that's the signal to not interrupt—sometimes for many, many hours at a time. Elly makes notes in her phone of anything she wants to talk about during these times and then busts out the list when I finish the current intensive research project.

- *Help your partner break down tasks into steps.* Autistic people are often perceived as being unwilling or even too stupid to do basic tasks like finding a job or picking up medications. If your partner is having trouble or getting lost in the minutiae, help them by breaking things down into steps. For example, when planning a meal, the first step might be to figure out if you should get takeout or cook. Then you can create a decision tree from there. Sometimes, when I'm incapacitated by attempting to decide which shoes to wear, it's helpful when Elly asks questions like "What will you be doing in these shoes?," "Are you going to see other people?," and "Will it be raining?" When tidying, accumulated piles can be sorted to make them neater and easier to put away. I once had a roommate who said, "If you can clean one square foot each day, it gets done and doesn't feel pointless." And she was right. Breaking tasks down into steps engages our brains and helps us find even more efficient ways of achieving these goals.

- *Understand that your partner's decision-making process is different from yours.* What seems like depression or sloppiness might be an informed, logical decision to your partner. When I walk in the door at the end of the day, I am exhausted, and I take off my clothes and let them lie where they fall. It's not about lack of caring or motivation; it's a functional system that works so that I can find them later. When Elly asked me to put them on my chair in the bedroom for the next day, I was willing and able, even if I didn't see the point. However, we later had to add a clause to this rule: "unless Joe is too exhausted to take these additional steps, in which case the clothes go wherever." This was how I communicated that exhaustion despite masking. Developing this kind of understanding helps the actions no longer feel personal and provides a way to interface with each other's physical and emotional states.

- *Understand why your partner bumps into things, loses balance, and drops stuff.* Autistic people often have difficulty with proprioception, or the ability to judge distances and to know how one's body relates to other objects. This results in mishaps like spilling a beverage because we attempted to set it on the edge of the counter or missing the pant legs and neckholes when trying to put our clothes on. I struggle the most with proprioception when bending over to tie my shoes—and now exclusively wear shoes without laces! You might want to do more of the handling of fragile items, but you don't really need to do anything differently except be patient, don't get overly attached to anything made of glass, and keep a dustpan handy.

- *Do not interrupt your partner's routines.* Routines are the glue that holds us together. They show us stability in the world and that some things are not hopeless. I wake up in the morning and my routine before I sit down takes exactly 15 minutes. I load the dishwasher, clear the sink, perform one monthly tidying project, and prepare two ounces of yerba maté for myself and food for my service dog. I move everything I need near my chair, do two hours of work, and then watch TV or listen to a podcast. By the time Elly wakes up, I am ready for socialization. For autistic people, breaking routines and expectations borders on traumatic. To not find something where we left it is deeply upsetting. Others' mistakes are inconceivable to us—we can't put ourselves in someone else's situation, so it's impossible to understand how they could have made the mistakes they did. Diagnosis made this much less upsetting for me as I began to understand what was going on and could learn to let go and forgive. Sometimes one of your partner's routines is going to involve organizing something in a very particular and time-consuming way, like loading boxes into the car in the optimal configuration, sorting a month's worth of pills, or putting all the pens in the house in order of color and size. Build extra time into your scheduling estimations for this to be completed.

- *Understand that autistic people struggle to see patterns at first, but once they do, they excel at pattern recognition.* Autistics have weak central coherence, or the ability to relate one concept to another. Weak central coherence is similar to executive function problems, and it's why we might get in an argument in the afternoon and then not understand why you don't want to have sex later. We have moved on, even if you haven't. You might need to connect the dots out loud for us sometimes, which will not be easy when you're feeling frustrated and misunderstood. However, once we understand a pattern, we are unstoppable in our ability to comprehend its nuances and navigate it. For instance, Elly once pointed out to me that we had gotten in a fight the night before every long trip we took together. Once she said this, it never happened again.

- *Make a list together of what feels good for each of you.* In a difficult situation, what do you each want and need? It's very likely that the ways in which you and your partner each want to be taken care of after a bad day, before a stressful event, during a hectic season, during an illness, or during a tragedy are very different from each other. For example, in moments of crisis, autistic people have trouble understanding that the mere presence of a partner can be calming for an allistic person—because that isn't logical. Autistic people think in terms of things that we can *do*, and while it feels good to help, it doesn't make sense that we are helping just by standing there and holding you. Tell us what you need in the form of clear actions that we can take, and you'll find that we perform astonishingly well. On the other hand, your autistic person might not have ever felt comfortable letting you know that when they are having a hard time, being alone in a quiet, dark room with the door closed is exactly what they need, and that letting you hold and "comfort" them is adding to their stress and delaying their recovery.

- *Don't assume they aren't doing equal work.* In almost any discussion of autistic-allistic relationships, there seems to be an assumption that the relationship will be unequal, and specifically that the allistic person is going to have more skills and do more work to make up for the autistic person's supposed deficits. This is true sometimes, but the reverse is also likely to be true. Add this to the mix: for many autistic people, much of the work they put into the relationship may not be as visible or appreciated—or even, once you sit down and talk about it, necessary. This work can include the exhausting emotional labor of masking or the mental work that goes into deeply considering a social situation or dynamic and problem solving around it. The more the allistic partner can learn to understand and remove some of these burdens, the more their autistic partner will be able to avoid burnout and have the bandwidth for different relationship work, including decision making, chores, and management of the social calendar. But first, one of you has to notice this work and bring it up. Then it's way easier to be like, "Babe, I don't need you to smile and nod and act super interested in my day right when you get home from work and you need to decompress. I want to tell you about my day, but I can wait until after dinner when we're both more relaxed."

HOUSEKEEPING

In any relationship, you need to balance each other's needs and abilities. Nobody in a relationship is ever going to get to do *only* things they enjoy, but as you divide your work, you are both going to be frustrated if you end up with the wrong relationship jobs. If one of you is terrible at filling out complicated paperwork, it probably doesn't make sense to have that person do the household's taxes every year. If someone burns everything they cook, they're probably not the best choice for regularly preparing dinner (though they might be great at ordering takeout!).

Elly here. How many beautiful relationships have been brought down by disagreements about housework? I have trouble thinking of any time I have ever been more frustrated with Joe than when I asked for tea grounds to be dumped into the compost container instead of the sink drain. I thought it was a reasonable request, but Joe disagreed, and my hackles went right up. There were raised voices, there were tears, there was walking away until everyone was calmer. Once that calmer state was achieved, we were able to hear each other and agree on an arrangement that suited both of our needs, abilities, and tolerances for encounters with decomposing organic matter.

I mean, housework seems to be difficult and loaded for *any* couple. We're bringing our baggage from our families and past relationships, maybe our assumptions about gender (and gender inequality), all our fears about what kind of person we are and how other people will see us, our insecurities about our relationship power dynamics, and our childhood expectations about our idyllic adult relationships, and we're directing all of this with laser focus on the question of how our dirty plates should get clean.

Add neurodiversity into the mix and that's an even more potent recipe for conflict—though considering limitations can also make some things simpler. If your partner can't handle the smells coming from the dishwasher when the dishes are dirty, then duh, they should not be the one loading it; but unloading it and putting everything in its rightful place might be just fine, or even super satisfying, for them. If they've got poor motor control and are prone to dropping things, maybe dishes are something you handle, or maybe you switch to plastic plates. This isn't to say that your partner shouldn't manage an equitable part of the load, and most important is the biggest question on all our minds when it comes to the division of household labor: Is it fair?

Like with every other challenge discussed in this book, the solution is to abandon expectations and talk about practicalities. Autism doesn't affect ability or willingness to take out the trash, at least not in any universal way, but it may affect your partner in ways you'll never know if you don't ask. Assuming that the laundry is piling up because your partner is autistic is just as bad as assuming it's because they're lazy or they don't respect you. But if you can find a place of calm from which to ask genuine questions and listen to the answers, you may learn that your partner hasn't noticed the laundry buildup, the dryer sheets make their nose itch, they put off folding laundry because you got mad at them once for doing it wrong, or laundry has traumatic associations for them. Or maybe they think folding laundry isn't a great use of their time and would prefer—as Joe did prior to this relationship—accumulating a wardrobe that can last three to six months before laundry is necessary and then spending a whole day washing everything (without folding, as there is little benefit to doing so) and forever grabbing the clean underwear from the top of the pile on the laundry table.

If your preferences are different, you'll need to negotiate. Maybe they'll wash the laundry and you'll fold it. Maybe when they hear from you how much the laundry mountain stresses you out, or that it brings up your own bad memories, or that one of your core values is keeping things orderly, they'll see that as a good reason to make an extra effort. Maybe you can meet each other halfway. Maybe you'll try it their way. Or maybe laundry is in your domain.

If your housework problems are really intractable or there are areas where you both have significant barriers or aversions, and if you can afford to, you could hire someone else to do your mopping, laundry, or grocery shopping. If this is a mutually agreeable solution, it could be a game-changer. And this outsourcing doesn't have to be managed by the person who usually does the thing. At one point about a decade ago, I got completely overwhelmed and burnt out on doing all the cooking and meal planning. Joe was too ill to take on that labor at the time but was able to organize a trade arrangement with a friend who could drop off a few meals a week. Everyone's needs were met according to their abilities. But be aware that if you're outsourcing the problem area instead of hashing out what's really going on, that same friction is going to pop right back up somewhere else.

Whatever you do, don't assign your partner chores and then get mad when they don't do them the way you want. You're not their parent. Talk about it. Try stuff, see how it goes, and talk about it again. If you can figure out, together, something as loaded as where to put shoes after taking them off, then your relationship is ready for any challenge life throws at you. Talking things over is guaranteed to bring some surprises to light. Maybe your partner feels sick from the fumes of the bathroom cleaner you use. Maybe they actually like doing laundry and would be happy to take it over. Maybe they have a romantic fantasy of hand-washing and drying the dishes together after dinner. Maybe they struggle with daily upkeep, but are great at regular deep cleans, taxes and financial planning, travel planning, removing the dead mouse that you found in the basement, setting up new appliances, organizing the bathroom, creating functional systems for how tasks are managed, taking care of the dog, coordinating childcare, and working with contractors.

Another possibility is your partner could be a lot neater than you in some or all areas, have rigid expectations for how things *need* to be done, and be stressed out by your mess and lack of predictable routine. If you're struggling to mesh with these needs and routines, talking things over and coming up with solutions that work for both of you is forever the way forward. Take a break if either of you gets upset, but come back to the discussion. If your negotiations end with them being the one taking on the bulk of the household management, make it your business to ensure that you're contributing to the relationship in other ways that feel equitable to you both.

It's most probable that you each see your own system and habits as the most functional and are trying hard to accommodate each other (or win each other over to your way). Years into our relationship, I learned to my chagrin that Joe really struggles when things are moved. Furniture, a pair of headphones, whatever. Apparently it's like walking into an unfamiliar room in a new house. I love to put things away, and this is an area where it's so hard to see Joe's perspective. I just can't train myself to see "dropped on the table" as "put away," whereas Joe can spend a frustrating 10 minutes looking for a pen that I have put into the pen cup on the counter where, logically to my mind, it belongs, and where I know I'll look next time I need a pen. It's a source of stress for both of us. But it's not something we fight about—we accommodate each other because we trust each other. Neither of us takes a misplaced pen as a sign that the other person doesn't respect or care about our feelings. And trust and respect are almost always the core issue in most housework disputes.

In some situations, more than 50% of the housework could end up on your plate. This might be okay.[20] Consider what you know about your partner, what they contribute to the relationship otherwise, what difficulties they have, and where you might budge on your own standards and preferences. Do you see and respect the work they *are* putting in? Do you take on all the household decision making along with the chores, or do you leave space for that to be shared? Is your relationship reciprocal, do you feel respected and generally not taken advantage of, and are you able to effectively talk over difficult things, solve problems, and make decisions together? Is this problem with housework a dealbreaker in its own right? Is it indicative of bigger, unresolvable problems in your relationship, or is it reminding you of problems in your past that have nothing to do with this relationship? If everything else is legitimately good, consider simply choosing to accept responsibility for doing the things you need to be comfortable at home. Framing it as your own choice, rather than something your partner is imposing on you, can make housework way less of a chore.

---

20 In her book *How to Keep House While Drowning*, neurodivergent therapist and mom KC Davis recommends focusing less on whether you're doing equal work in your partnership and more on making sure each partner has equal opportunities for genuine rest.

GIFT GIVING

While autistic people are better with actions than words, they can have a very hard time with gift giving, as it's so emotionally complex. Your autistic partner is likely to put a *lot* of thought into gifts, and less likely to tell you that they are doing so.

Elly here. Joe noticed right away that I like chocolate and spent the first year of our relationship observing my taste in chocolate and asking specific questions, resulting in a series of gifts of chocolates that were more and more delicious and that I never would have found for myself. These were all delivered completely without fanfare.

Any kind of traditional gift-giving occasion may be loaded though. The two of us simply do not share gifts for birthdays or holidays. Instead, we get each other presents when we find something that we believe would make the other happier. This removes a tremendous amount of pressure and, we believe, results in much better and more useful gifts. This is not unique to interabled relationships, of course, and many couples resolve this issue simply by sharing wishlists with each other and using that as a starting point.

Years ago, on the Wrong Planet forums for autistic people, an autistic person told a story about how his wife had requested spontaneous gifts, so he spent the following month observing her and making a list of small things that she would appreciate. Then he wrote a computer program to prompt him, at random intervals, to obtain one of these gifts and surprise her. This is a perfect example of how an autistic person can use their own creativity and ingenuity to meet their partner's needs.

Meanwhile, I have learned that Joe doesn't particularly need or even like to be surprised by gifts. There are some spontaneous gifts that will always go over well, like an iced tea, a new travel cup, or something cute that I found in a free box, meaning there's no obligation to keep it for longer than it takes to appreciate the thoughtfulness. But with anything more complicated, I ask first. Then Joe gets a gift that is optimally useful and gets to enjoy the positive feelings associated with receiving a gift even before actually getting it.

Joe here. I have received many gifts that only serve to illustrate how little the giver knows about my inner life. Principally, people give me things that they think that I should like or even give me things after I specifically told them that I have no use for those things.[21] A 2022 study about gift giving found that the most likely way to make the gift receiver happy is to ask them what they want in advance. Any autistic person can confirm that asking beforehand is the most logical approach.

SEX

For autistic people, sex can be complicated by aversion to touch and the risk of sensory assaults. For some, sex is the perfect sensory experience, while for other autistic people, sex is horribly unpleasant because the many sights, sounds, smells, tastes, and sensations can be so intense that there is no room left for pleasure. While the studies are few, it does appear that among individuals with a formal diagnosis of autism, there is a higher instance of self-reported asexuality.

Of course, most autists fall somewhere in the middle. They enjoy sex but do have to account for some sensory overload. And, of course, many people under the asexuality umbrella aren't sex repulsed so much as they experience less sexual desire. If you suspect your partner is struggling with some aspect of physical intimacy,

21 The popular statistic on unwanted gifts is 40%, but that's just what is disclosed, so I'd venture a guess that it's closer to 65%.

figuring out how they see themselves best expressing their sexual self is an important start.

Most autistic people do want pleasure and sexual gratification, as complicated as this can be to achieve. Many autistic people experience mutism during sex due to overwhelm. Changing gears from previous activities to sex can also be a giant leap for autistic people. For these reasons, some autistic people *never* have sex, as the cons outweigh the pros. Others are never able to fully achieve the emotional "letting go" during sex and instead remain in their conscious bodies, making decisions rather than giving themselves over to the throes of passion. I (Joe) have dated numerous people who complained that my touch was robotic or even that the way that I would caress their back was too geometric and repetitive.

You can work together on making sex less of a complicated pleasure. If you find that your partner is having a hard time relaxing into sexual touch, one reliable technique is massaging them. It relaxes the body and distracts the mind. You may also find that you become much more comfortable during sex when your partner massages you. Be aware that, often, brushing lightly against an autistic person's skin is much more overwhelming and upsetting than a firm, confident touch. This is true for the same reason that weighted blankets are comforting. But you won't know unless you ask, and listen.

Since so much of sexual communication is playful and suggestive rather than direct, it can be very confusing to the autistic partner. Sometimes, the most helpful thing that you can do during sex is naming your tone, your feelings, and your needs, since your facial expressions, noises, and body language at these times can be incredibly difficult to interpret. Are you in pain or in ecstasy? Are you warming up or not feeling it? Are you teasing or wanting something? Do you need to script your partner's behavior or want them to always behave and approach the situation unpredictably to surprise you? When texting about sex, it's very important to use "tone tags," which are keys to understanding what you mean and when you are joking. This reduces possibilities for awkward and embarrassing miscommunication.

One lesson that can be learned from the BDSM community is talking very openly about *every last thing* and having very clear rules: "When you say this, we stop. When I say that, it means I'm enjoying this." The Organization for Autism Research has an online series of guides called Sex Ed for Self-Advocates that outlines many specific problems and solutions; it's aimed at younger people but could be helpful for people of any age. There are also various sex toys that can help with problems related to sensory assault and overwhelm. Toys that are used for playing with power, like blindfolds or noise-canceling headphones, can help manage sensory overload for your partner. Meanwhile, items such as wedge pillows and lube can help them feel more comfortably situated in their body and more receptive to your touch.

If your background has not been very queer, kinky, or sexually adventurous, you may find it deeply uncomfortable to talk about sex at all, either before, during, or after. It gets easier with practice, so approach it like any new thing you're learning. Also, be open to redefining what you think of as "sex." Assumptions you might have about types of touch, the sequence of events, interpersonal dynamics between partners, eye contact, and orgasms are all on the table for reconsideration. The only thing that matters is that you do what works for both you and your partner.

If your partner has developed an unreasonable or unhealthy view of roles during sex due to past experiences, explain how you feel about this and steer them back towards rescripting their view of sexual gratification. Use resources (books, articles, porn) that center the types of sex you enjoy having; this could involve, for example, an increased focus on foreplay and mutual satisfaction. Then let this media spark a discussion about what turns each of you on and what you don't like.

As you become more comfortable with each other, it's vital to continue to communicate verbally about sex. It's not how you see it done in the movies, but it makes it vastly more rewarding and you'll feel much closer to each other, which is really the point. Like any investment in life, improving your sex life takes time and patience, but you are equipping each other to understand, predict, and be attentive to the other's needs and wants. And like in all aspects of a relationship, becoming closer during sex is truly magical; there are few limits to what two determined people can accomplish together in bed.

LIFE MILESTONES

For many younger adults, a relationship is a hallmark of adulthood that involves a lot of expectations that were formed in childhood. In many ways, your adult relationships feel interwoven with other choices and milestones like college, marriage, owning a car, how you practice religion, where you live, having children, how you spend holidays, and plans for retirement. Sometimes, for better or worse, an autistic partner can offer newfound perspective on the privileges that these milestones imply. This is to say that something you take for granted, like owning a car, may not be feasible in terms of life structure, finances, or executive function for your partner, or it might just not make sense to them. Cars and driving come with a lot of complex, interconnected ideas, rules, and concerns that an allistic person might quickly become accustomed to but to which not all autistic people will want or be able to adjust. And cars are just the tip of the iceberg: adulthood has a strange way of monkey wrenching expectations. So when you're discussing your life goals and assumptions, it's better to frame these as ideals rather than set in stone. Think about whether each expectation or life goal is a need, a want, or an idea; consider which of these are *your* dreams and which of them are actually societal expectations or your parents' dreams for you.

Within the first year of our relationship, I (Joe) declared that marriage just didn't make *sense*. There were no tangible benefits. It was only involving the state in our love. This is not a popular point of view, and most allistics would likely interpret it as apprehension or fear of commitment—containing a meaning deeper than what is stated. Elly, however, was able to understand this point of view, accept it at face value, and come around to it quickly, instead of taking offense or seeing it as my own lack of commitment. I do see things a bit differently now and am very fortunate that Elly was able to listen and understand where I was coming from at that time. Because, as a result, our loyalty only gets stronger every day. The topic of marriage is revisited every few years, usually in a comedic manner. No actual advantages have been uncovered yet, and we receive the security that marriage offers in other ways, but the topic is still an open discussion 14 years later.

Other life milestones, like owning a home or car, graduating from college, having children, and planning for retirement are all things we have had to negotiate in various ways. I had already done the math on all of those things and determined that owning a home was the only one that penciled out. Elly agrees about car ownership not making any sense, but she had to think more about some of the others. I was willing to have children if that was important to her. At first, she said it was; but after a few years of inaction, she realized that the idea that she didn't necessarily have to reproduce had never occurred to her, and she was deeply relieved to have been given the space to come to the realization that she did not want to be a parent.

If you are the sort of person to be very attached to specific life milestones happening in a particular sequence and time frame, you may get the opportunity to question that attachment as you negotiate long-term plans with your autistic partner. Of course, they may be even more rigidly attached to these milestones than you. But also be prepared to have the institutions you believe in dissected and dismantled, and to be questioned about why things make sense, what the advantages are, and what is merely a product of unexamined expectations, upbringing, old baggage, or various insecurities.

PARENTING

Caring for yourself, your partner, and your relationship is already a big project—what about when there are dependents involved? Parenting is a huge topic, and one we don't have the experience to fully do justice to here, none of us having co-parented with an autistic partner.[22] But we want to acknowledge how bringing kids into your household can affect your relationship when there's autism in the mix.

Becoming a parent, especially to an infant, involves a lot of sensory stimulus, stress, overwhelm, increasingly complex social situations, disrupted routines, and basically everything specifically designed to push an autistic person beyond their ability to cope. So any coping skills and self-knowledge your partner can gain in advance will be a gift to themself, you, and especially your kids. You,

---

22 Faith's book *Woke Parenting*, coauthored with fellow parent and therapist Bonnie Scott, is worth reading for more wisdom about parenting and co-parenting through all the complexity of modern life.

an adult, understand when your partner freaks out or shuts down. Your kid doesn't, and may think it's their fault.

An autistic parent who is self-aware and has healthy strategies to manage their own life can be a great role model and teacher for kids, who themselves are easily overwhelmed and hugely reliant on routines and are learning every day about how to be a person in the world. And if any of your kids are autistic, it's even better for them to have a parent who can relate to their needs and point them on the way to growing up with self-acceptance.

I (Joe) raised a foster child and found that for children over six, most parenting comes down to listening, reasoning, expressing boundaries, and patiently offering exposition (yes, sometimes over and over and over again) about the current variety of available options. Fortunately, this is an area of communication where autistic people excel. And, speaking from experience, just about every autistic person that I know is very good at relating to children. Sometimes what's required is as simple as a firm boundary: "You have to wash your hands before you eat fruit even though that boy didn't" or "No, your co-parent doesn't let you stand on the counter either" or "We can go play with the dog in the park after you finish your homework" or "I'm too tired to play right now. Want to watch a movie?" or "I'm sorry that those other kids were making fun of you, that's really wrong and unfair. I think you're really awesome." In some situations, when the dynamic is much more complex, you can't always offer a full exposition and you have to stop at the boundary: "It's never okay to 'play doctor' with other kids." In other situations, the child has a genuine curiosity, so explaining things to them like you would to an adult can result in revelatory and humorous exchanges—such as the time that I calculated how many minutes it takes to print a book, and the child concluded that this was too long and he'd need to call the printer.

In most cases, since the child's strategy is to test boundaries until they find an acceptable path towards what they want, patience and rigidity are strengths here. The woman that co-parented the foster child with me would bring me in when the same boundary needed to be reinstated 10 or 20 times in a row, because I would neither lose my patience nor relent. If you lose your temper, the child has a small, Pyrrhic victory, so leaning on your autistic partner's strengths around consistency and justice can be helpful, both for providing additional perspective about what is going on and for communicating this effectively to the child.

Your autistic partner might need more time away from young kids or pets than feels reasonable or fair to you. Hopefully the skills we've talked about in the rest of this book will help you negotiate solutions to ensure that your kid gets all their needs met and the adults get at least enough of their needs met to survive, with the understanding that each phase in your kid's development will eventually be replaced by a new one with new challenges.

CHAPTER 5: YOUR LIFE TOGETHER IN SOCIETY

Sometimes, everything is going swimmingly in your private life and you get all of those warm feelings from the strength of your relationship. And then there's life outside your home.

Joe has told me (Elly) many times that going out in public without me typically results in worse treatment, sharing plenty of harrowing tales of interactions with strangers, including being petted, being told it wasn't safe to be out alone, being ignored by service providers, and even experiencing some attempted assaults. Going places together is a bit safer, but hardly perfect.

When Joe and I are together at home or on a quiet walk, autism is the last thing on my mind. In our conversations and the life we've built together, many disabling factors have been neutralized. But in a crowded public setting or when meeting someone new, it's the first thing on my mind. I can see the way strangers, waiters, cops, or colleagues respond to Joe, and that changes my outlook and behavior. I become alert for signs of miscommunication, prejudice, or danger. I try to project my respect for Joe in a more exaggerated way so that others will take my cue. I see interactions with others differently with Joe at my side—either because I'm more alert or because sometimes people show different sides of themselves when faced with a behavior or vibe that makes them uncomfortable. I can see more clearly that someone who I liked on first meeting is actually a little mean, or is trying to take advantage.

Surprisingly often, someone will be deferentially polite or friendly to me but completely ignore, dismiss, or be rude to Joe, who is standing right next to me. When we were first together, even when Joe pointed out what happened, I brushed these incidents off as an anomaly or misunderstanding. It wasn't until five years into our relationship, when we traveled to a conference together where I was a speaker, that we were faced with a series of really blatant incidents and I could no longer deny that this was in fact happening, not just at this conference but on a daily basis.

It was disorienting, like stepping into another dimension, and for a long time I kept discovering new aspects of this pattern that I'd previously been unable or unwilling to see. I was so angry, not least at myself for denying Joe's experience and abetting mistreatment. There was no coming back from this series of realizations, which ultimately led to a career move and some serious rethinking of who I wanted in my life—all of which made my life much less chaotic and more fulfilling.

Perhaps you've had similar realizations in your own relationship, or perhaps you're only just now beginning to think about how your partner might be treated differently out in the world. In this chapter, we offer guidance on how you and your partner can better navigate social situations and power structures beyond the boundaries of your relationship. Facing discrimination every day is exhausting, and while that isn't something you can entirely prevent, understanding what is happening and being able to support your partner can make all the difference in their ability to negotiate the biases, threats, and absurd demands the world throws at them.

SHARED SOCIAL LIFE

If you open just about any resource about autism, it will extensively discuss how to make neurotypical people comfortable. This reflects a power structure that operates like any other—by prioritizing those who already have the cards stacked in their favor over those who are vulnerable. Think about this as you and your partner socialize together, choose friends, and allow people into your inner circle.

Like in any relationship, it's okay to have your own friends as individuals as well as friends that you share as a couple. But there are other things to consider.

- *It's frankly just too difficult to have a lot of friends as an autistic person.* It's exhausting and confusing, and it takes away from pursuing one's meaning and purpose—maybe one or two friends are happy to talk *only* about that, but most people have different interests and priorities. Because of this, for many years Joe would ignore friends for months or years at a time and then try to re-engage after a long period of silence. For many of these friends, this was not acceptable. All of these dynamics make autistic people's partners and the friends they do have much more essential. Sometimes it's important to maintain closer communication. In other cases, it's important to find people operating on the same rhythms, who can pick up and set down the relationship at convenient intervals.

- *Be a buffer as needed.* Ask your partner when they would benefit from you acting as a buffer to the outside world. At various times in the relationship, you will need to be both a social buffer and a translator. If you're doing something new, give your partner an honest but positive overview of exactly what will happen that day. If your partner has severe social impairment, try scripting all of the encounters before they happen. Help your date understand other people's strange behavior, as it's difficult for them to see the reaction that they are bringing out in others.

- *Be on the same page about how to handle awkwardness.* Some interabled partnerships thrive on secret codes for communicating social cues in public. Your partner may start talking about things that others aren't interested in, and you might agree on a phrase to indicate when to tone that down. Many autistics struggle with "voice modulation," meaning they don't understand when they are talking inappropriately loudly for the environment or situation. Your autistic partner cannot perceive an emotional iceberg in the room—such as the unspoken tension between two people or someone acting very uncomfortable—and may benefit from having it pointed out to them later. Some autistic people haplessly manufacture an awkward situation involving politics or religion in a way that creates a time bomb. Helping them walk away from disaster before the relationship is harmed can be important. On the other hand, Elly is allergic to secret codes and can't see a way to use them that wouldn't feel condescending, not to mention deeply obvious to any observer. Her rule here is to let most awkwardness go in the moment. She and Joe can talk about it later, if it's a pattern of socially unadept behavior or a misunderstanding that seems worth dissecting (or maybe just laughing about together!). If a situation seems to warrant intervention, Elly tries to make it super straightforward and not assume that she has the ultimate read on it. For instance, she will very occasionally, in an informal social setting, say, "You're speaking super loudly" in the same friendly, low-key way she would let someone know they had a poppy seed stuck in their teeth. Then Joe will say, "What? I can't hear you," and it just becomes part of their normal banter. Sometimes more information creates the opportunity for informed consent, meaning the autistic partner can freely choose to continue down a given path. Maybe they *intend* to be speaking loudly for effect, or maybe they actively want to bring up a controversial subject. If Elly sees a serious misunderstanding brewing, she might step in to ask a clarifying question along the lines of "Are we all on the same page about this?" or "I think I heard you say X, is that right?" But most of the time, she just doesn't worry about it. If someone is perturbed by loud talking or a missed social cue, that's on them. No codes needed. Figure out what's right for your relationship, agree on it, and proceed towards a happy life together. The vital thing here is *not to blame the autistic partner* when a social interaction goes awry. It takes two to create any situation, and often the other party is the awkward one or at least equally responsible.

- *Be on your partner's side when it comes to sensory overload.* While autistic people sometimes don't know how loud they're speaking, it's just as likely that someone else speaking loudly is going to overwhelm their senses. For an autistic person to explain how their sensory issues affect them can be embarrassing if not humiliating. Having a supportive loved one as an advocate is enormously helpful. If crowds, noises, smells, or light are a problem, your partner is going to get sick of explaining that certain social activities are unpleasant or even traumatic; other people tend to not even notice the stimulus, whereas it's the first thing the autistic person thinks about when these activities are suggested. Sometimes you can help by asking to turn the music down or seat your group somewhere where the lights or smells are not so intense or direct. Even when stimulation cannot be completely eradicated, it's the thought that counts and makes someone feel loved. Honestly and briefly explaining your partner's sensory issues is the best way to raise awareness, receive support and empathy, and prevent people from escalating these problems. Talk to your partner about which explanations feel best for them. For example, they may not want you to say they're autistic, but they might be comfortable with you saying, "Joe has a neurological condition that makes noises like this headache inducing; we're gonna tap out now, but thank you so much for inviting us!"

- *Discuss what is going on around you emotionally.* Your relationship will never be boring, because you will always have very different reads on any social situation to compare after the fact. Once, Joe, Elly, and a coworker were interviewing a job candidate. They told her what they were offering and she responded, "I'm going to have to crunch some numbers." Joe took her at her word, while the other two interviewers and another nearby worker, who was not even looking at her at the time, *all* reported her visible discomfort and "the mood changing in the room." She was being polite and they could all "feel it." They all insisted that they wouldn't hear from her again, whereas Joe believed that they should wait a few days for her to crunch those numbers. She wrote back a week later to say that the offer didn't meet her needs . . . so everyone was correct. Tell your partner when something just happened emotionally or socially that you think they might have missed. Ask how they interpreted it. You'll probably both learn something!

- *Help your partner understand social cause and effect.* Instrumental interaction means connecting with someone to meet a specific objective, like when you click a button on a website to achieve an intended outcome. Autistic people are very good at this when the objective is clear and mechanical. Beyond that, autistic people struggle with cause and effect. In 1993, I (Joe) watched a movie with a date and she used my flannel shirt as a pillow while we lay on the floor next to each other. The following week, she cheated on me with her ex. I haven't let anyone use my shirt as a pillow for the past 30 years. This is an example of difficulty distinguishing between correlation and causation. Obviously, her putting her head on my shirt isn't what caused the cheating, but that's how the wound is impressed on my brain. An autistic partner will draw inaccurate conclusions like this from past experiences. They will avoid those behaviors in the future, even if they were just isolated incidents. You can work together with your partner to show them that these wounds can heal and that some people are safe to trust in.

- *Help your partner to understand the gravity and impact of their choices without dictating them.* The impulse, even for absolute strangers, is to attempt to dictate choices for autistic people: "It's not safe for you to be here." "Don't do that." "You can't use scissors." This impulse is born of the assumption that autistic people could never have sufficient information to make decisions about how to direct their lives in the way that other people do. It can be difficult to step back and say, "When you say that, it's going to be interpreted this way by the listener" instead of "Don't say that!" But, fundamentally, this is the difference between an independent relationship and a dependent one.

- *Give your partner time to adjust.* Autistic people are just as likely to enjoy new things as anyone else, but the first time can be very difficult. Give your partner some familiar comforts and ideas of what to expect, research in advance, and maybe find a menu, reviews, a virtual video tour, or most importantly, an opportunity to back out if it's too much. Not all social settings are equal: Static settings like a train station are organized and predictable. A cocktail party on the other hand is fluid, free form, and unpredictable. A fluid setting creates a much greater cognitive load. Your partner can probably participate in these settings sometimes if the activities are important to you, but it will take a tremendous toll on them. They will likely not enjoy themselves. But we do things for people that we love; it's part of any relationship.

- *Stopping a meltdown or shutdown does not help your partner.* If your partner's ability to cope is overwhelmed, it's very important to stand back and let a meltdown happen— especially if it's in public. Try to prevent injury, damage, or a social situation that could get your partner in further trouble, but do not attempt to stifle the meltdown. Likewise, if your partner is shutting down, it's important to give them space and avoid adding more stimulus. With suitable trust, time, and accommodation, you will watch overwhelm and meltdowns disappear completely.

By checking in after social encounters—good and bad—you can get a sense of how the situation felt for your partner, what they missed, what they enjoyed, what was painful, and what you two should do differently next time—if there is a next time for that type of encounter!

FRIENDS AND FAMILY

So you may understand and accept your autistic partner as they are. But friends, family members, coworkers, and acquaintances may not be so lucky, and they may not be open to such understanding or acceptance either.

You and your partner may need to help the people close to you process a new autism diagnosis. Unless you're exceptionally close to your families, consider not making them the first people you tell. Lauren Ober, in her podcast *The Loudest Girl in the World*, walks listeners through her coming-out process as an adult diagnosed in her 40s. First she told select close friends, who were of course wonderfully supportive. Bolstered by this, she moved on to telling less-close friends and acquaintances, learning from their wide range of responses and her own occasional awkwardness in handling those responses. All this practice finally made her feel more ready to tell her parents and siblings.

Family members are maybe the trickiest people to tell. Lauren Ober advises preparing the ground by first telling your family that you have some big news about yourself. (This also makes it harder to back out due to nerves.) If you and your partner will be telling family members together, make a plan, and decide on who will do most of the telling, how much to tell, and how to handle any potential reaction, like enthusiastic support, curiosity, denial, mansplaining, catastrophizing, or conspiracy theories about vaccines. You know, the normal range of responses to any big news. Make a list of ways in which family members may respond and a plan for each. This way, you'll feel more in control of the situation, no matter how it unfolds. Also have an exit plan, and treat yourself to ice cream or something afterward to celebrate doing a hard thing.

If your partner's diagnosis was long ago, you may instead be dealing with how family members already treat them. Do their parents try to protect them from the world? Do their siblings leave them out of family decisions? Do your parents embrace your partner's differences, or do they disapprove and think you've settled? Learning more about autism and developing your communication skills and boundaries as a result may lead to some heartbreaking realizations for both of you. Whether or not you think some of these dynamics might be rooted in family members' attitudes about autism, it might be worth having a conversation with your partner about identifying opportunities to shift these dynamics, even if just subtly. Maybe, with your partner's consent, you can start standing up for them when they are overlooked or veiled comments are made about their abilities. Maybe you can agree to relieve your holiday season stress by 2000% every year by skipping Thanksgiving at Uncle Bob's.

If you're introducing your new partner to family for the first time, you can decide together whether or not to brief the family on autism beforehand. This is so particular to each situation that it's hard to give advice on it. You don't want to come across as setting a low bar or, worse, excusing presumed bad behavior in advance. Whatever you decide, it's generally a good idea to avoid overwhelm by introducing your partner to small groups of family members gradually rather than at the family reunion or a noisy birthday party. Follow the same playbook as the one for coming out and start with the people who are most likely to be warmly accepting, even if they aren't the closest family members; take heart and practical lessons from those encounters. You can also get advice and support from trusted family members on approaching more difficult ones (for instance, by asking your sister, who has met your date and loves them, for advice on whether and how to broach the topic with Mom).

In other cases, your role is in explaining to your partner that others don't mean harm. A friend told Joe that an autistic cousin was angry at him for years because the friend wouldn't spend an entire wedding sitting at the bar with the cousin and preferred instead to spend his time talking with the rest of the family. It's easy to see this story from both sides. The autist is thinking, "Alright! I bonded with someone in this awkward social situation! I win!" and Joe's friend is thinking, "I can't be chained to talking to you all night." In situations like these, your partner may need assurance that people did not mean harm or disrespect and that new situations often trigger old trauma.

Another consideration in your relationships with friends and family members is that once you've learned about autism, you may start to see autism everywhere. Take it from Elly: resist the urge to inform anyone of your guess that they are autistic unless you have a close, trusting relationship and know you are both able to handle emotionally activating conversations.

BE YOUR PARTNER'S ADVOCATE

Whether you're on a public street, out with friends, or at the family holiday dinner table, it's only going to be a matter of time before you witness someone treating your partner poorly.

If autism is new to the conversation, you will find yourself frequently in the awkward position of learning just how ignorant most people are about autism. I (Joe) kept my autism secret for seven years after diagnosis, because for the first few weeks after my initial diagnosis, each time that I told someone about it they would stare at me blankly and say some variation of "I don't think so. My cousin has autism and he's nothing like you." I grew tired of this immediately. As the partner of an autistic person, you are in a unique position to come equipped with facts and credibility in order to educate people about what autism is, how it manifests, and how unique it can look in each person. Ask your partner what they want from you in this capacity, and decide what you're willing to do and say. Do they want a public advocate? A private one? Someone to say something when neurophobic slurs are uttered in their presence? Or just someone to commiserate with later?

The largest factor here is that so little research has been done about autistic adults that most people's point of reference is children. Many doctors and parents literally expect us to grow out of it or die in the closet. By showcasing a happy and successful relationship, you can challenge these expectations and help demonstrate a more realistic version of an autistic adult.

However, as always, the autistic partner should be the one to make the decision about when, if ever, to disclose their autism. Disclosure can be important for two reasons: First, without understanding autism, people will pathologize your partner as a selfish asshole (or far worse); this conversation opens the door to educate other people about autism. Second, hiding your partner's autism can defray trust. However, sometimes this is a necessary compromise because of the discrimination that your partner might face following disclosure. Even though autistic people are a protected class of people with disabilities, this does not prevent people from being rude or making our lives insufferable. Together, you can build acceptance and education, but only if you're both on the same page about this and it won't compromise your partner's well-being.

When people pick on your partner, you may choose to step in and resolve the tension, even if your partner can't see what's happening. Sometimes this is as simple as a restaurant server ignoring your partner in favor of talking with you. Sometimes it's more outward, like your family talking shit about your partner out of their earshot. Sometimes it's someone in your friend group isolating your partner from social opportunities. Sometimes it's a police officer harassing your partner for being themself in public. In each of these cases, the best thing to do is simultaneously speak truthfully about the situation and flatteringly about your partner, while reframing what's happening. This can sound like anything from "I love her because she's so thoughtful and funny" to "Is there a problem here?" or even "If *this* is your biggest concern, I'm happy for you." If you don't do this in the moment, you are subtly condoning the other person's behavior as acceptable, and everyone sees that. Show that it's not acceptable. It will make you and your partner closer. And it bears repeating that you don't need to disclose your partner's neurology in order to make your partner make sense. Instead, you can reframe their actions and choices.

Autistic people cannot always tell whether someone has their best interests at heart or not. If your partner feels shunned, harmed, or hurt by the way that someone else is treating them, deal with the situation without denying their experience. Even if you don't have a strong sense that your partner was wronged, if your partner has expressed feelings about being ostracized in the past, support them. Taking sides with a bully (such as a police officer, abusive family member, or otherwise disruptive person) will drive you and your partner apart. As in any dynamic where privilege is involved, it is much more likely that you cannot see the transgression or microaggression because your life doesn't require you to think about it. To claim that you've never been bullied by this person is like a white person saying they've never been on the receiving end of racism. Of course they haven't!

Like with any advocacy, it can be easy to go overboard. Jumping to your partner's defense doesn't need to become your full-time job, and it's probably healthier for you, them, and the relationship if you have some boundaries around that. The simplest way to know when you should step in or say something is to ask your partner. If it's awkward to ask in the moment, then debrief later. "Was it okay that I said that to your sister, or would you rather have spoken for yourself or just let it go?" is a good conversation starter. Or "I was really uncomfortable with how Billy was mimicking your voice at board game night, and I wish I'd spoken up. Should I have?" You're also allowed to have boundaries in these situations—even if your partner generally wants you to speak up in their defense, there may be specific circumstances or moments when you aren't up for it. In these cases, it can be comforting for you to say something later; you never know when something hurtful is causing your partner to quietly stew, and simply bringing it up can help them feel better.

When you first start talking about advocating for your partner, you'll likely have a lot of these conversations as you both figure out your own and each other's needs, but soon it will become second nature and you'll only need to check in occasionally. These conversations will bring you closer together and you'll never be bored.

DEALING WITH ARMED AUTHORITIES

In some cases, the stakes are much higher. Due to the way that police are trained, they often view autistic people's basic behaviors as red flags. In the worst cases, this could prove fatal for your partner, so it's crucial to understand the ways in which autistic people are discriminated against by law enforcement.

Police are usually not trained to interact with autistic people, and autistic people can provoke fear in police officers and activate their fight response. I (Joe) have lost count of how many times I've been harassed by the police for being odd. In one case an officer pulled me over on my bike because a house had been robbed in the direction that I was coming from. I explained to him in mathematical terms that I couldn't be the suspect because I would have had to break the land speed record to have made it as far as I did. He responded with "I'm just doing my job. Don't be so annoyed." I wasn't annoyed; I was countering his suspicions with facts. In another case, a routine traffic stop was dragged out for hours because I was "acting suspicious" and the police "knew" that I was "hiding something." About twice per year I am stopped by police for no reason while riding my bike to work before dawn. It might sound like a stretch to say that I know I'm lucky to be alive, but it's also true.

In 2016, a high-profile case in Florida involved a 26-year-old autistic man, Arnaldo Rios Soto. Arnaldo had left his facility and was sitting in the street playing with a toy truck. A passing motorist saw him and called the police, claiming that he might have a gun. When police arrived at the scene, an officer shot at Arnaldo but instead hit his behavioral therapist, Charles Kinsey. Arnaldo's experience is a much more probable outcome for an autistic adult than, for example, the experience of the character Sam on the TV show *Atypical*, who has a middle-class family and a supportive community with endless time and resources to devote to him. While much of the brilliance of *Atypical* is its ability to isolate autism from trauma, it's not a realistic example of what happens when an autistic person has a meltdown on public transportation or stalks his former therapist. Despite supportive parents, Arnaldo has been mistreated institutionally for almost his entire life, which created a series of behaviors related to both his isolation and repeated trauma.

The podcast *Aftereffect* does a magnificent job of humanizing Arnaldo and demonstrating what happens to autistic adults in institutions. One thing that it's important to understand is that autistic people are shot by police frequently because our mannerisms and behaviors are interpreted as suspicious, not because we are violent or uncooperative. Autistic people often do not understand social expectations in an encounter with police or simply don't respond fast enough.

Worse than my many encounters with police is knowing that there would likely be no repercussions if any of these police officers hurt or killed me. Jonathan Aledda, the officer who shot and wounded Arnaldo's therapist, was initially found guilty of culpable negligence, but his conviction was overturned in 2022 due to an issue with the trial proceedings. In many other cases, the officer merely has to testify that they were afraid for their life to justify harming and even murdering another individual.

You can pick your battles with friends, family, or random strangers. But when your partner is dealing with police, security guards, or other armed individuals, this can be a life-or-death situation and your intervention may be needed.

If you've never been in a position to be personally concerned about police violence before, well, now you are. And you may need to shift your perspective considerably. Discuss with your partner ways you can help minimize their exposure to police and security in the course of daily life. Consider in what situations you would call 911. What about the police non-emergency line? Are there police-free (or at least non-police-first) alternatives in your area, like 988 or local hotlines for mental health emergencies? If you aren't sure what your options are, you can call 211 in most parts of the U.S., ask for referrals, and program those numbers into your phone before there's an emergency. Are there some situations in which you previously would not have hesitated to involve authorities but in which you now wouldn't involve them at all, like when you have a noise complaint?

Here's one very real scenario. The people who live across the street from us have regular late-night parties with a live band that go late enough to overlap with my waking hours. The first time this happened on a weeknight, neighbors organized to all make noise complaints. Elly realized that it was likely that the police would show up, find me sitting on the porch, register that something wasn't right, and manufacture an incident. She tried to explain to the neighbors that calling the police could have unexpected negative consequences that they were not considering because of their privilege. While the police are perceived as a protective force for some percentage of the population, mileage and experience varies wildly.

For any likely scenario where physical harm could be involved, talk it over, discussing what you and your partner would each do. Program relevant numbers into your phone, and if you're feeling extra proactive, write down your safety plan somewhere where you both can easily access and update it. Get to know your neighbors so that they will be more likely to understand your partner's autistic behaviors as normal and be less likely to call the police themselves.

What if you and your partner are approached by police, security, or armed randos when you're at an event, out on the street, driving, or at work? Have a plan for this. The least amount of engagement possible is safest, so first step back and see if they'll just pass right by. If they approach your partner, you might choose to simply be alert and have your phone ready to record while your partner handles the situation.[23] Or maybe you'll step right up and do the talking. (This is why it's good to have a predetermined plan, so you know what support your partner actually wants from you in this situation and don't end up manufacturing more suspicion through your contradictory actions.)

---

23 The ACLU has an app for filming police interactions. If you live in an area where the authorities are known to take your phone from your hand and delete the video you are taking, you may want to download this app. It uploads the video to the ACLU's secure cloud storage so it cannot be erased from your phone.

What if things start to escalate—the officer is repeating themself and raising their voice, your partner is showing signs of imminent meltdown, or people's expressions are angry? Now is really the time to step in, no matter the usual plan.

"Can I help you, officer?" said with quiet authority can help draw focus away from your partner while de-escalating a tense situation. Channel Obi-Wan Kenobi in *Star Wars* with his confident "These aren't the droids you're looking for." Remain calm and be painfully polite. Your goal isn't to be right or point out obvious absurdities and injustices; it's a safe exit for you and your partner. Keep your voice level and slow, your expression neutral. Do not argue—nodding and agreeing is your best strategy. "I understand" and "of course" may be all you need to say. "Can you explain what problem you see here?" might be a good way to ask the officer to walk backwards through how they arrived at an erroneous conclusion, or it might just get you yelled at. Another good option is to ask, "Are we being detained or are we free to go?" While still being respectful, you are demonstrating that you have an awareness of what the officer is and isn't legally able to do. It is also helpful to look up the specifics in your state regarding what information you are legally required to share if questioned. For example, in Texas, you are not required to show your driver's license or state ID to a police officer unless you are carrying a handgun, are driving, or are actually being arrested.

If you have a certain level of privilege and you know how to wield it, this is a time to do so. Maybe you allow just a hint of impatience to creep into your manner, a mere suggestion that you have the influence and willpower to make things very unpleasant for them if they misstep. Or maybe your superpower is shifting the narrative of the interaction to frame it as just a friendly, breezy misunderstanding. Maybe you've got the right background and vibe to buddy up with the cops, position yourself on their side, and move everyone along. You know what you've got, so work it.

Make sure your phone is in your hand and be ready to record. Rehearse variations on such encounters in your mind (or role-play them) so that you're ready to maintain that calm voice of clarity that will reassure the people with guns that you have everything under control and their "services" are not needed.

Of course, you can't be by your partner's side all of the time, and they are quite likely going to get harassed by the police when alone rather than with you (see Joe's experiences above). If dealing with authority figures is particularly activating, it may be helpful to have some kind of card that your partner carries with them that explains their diagnosis and their responses to overwhelm. For example, they may go mute due to anxiety, and the card will explain that to the officer in question, lessening the appearance of hostility. (But they should also be careful when reaching for this card so an officer doesn't assume they're going for a weapon.) If your partner carries medications with them, it is also helpful to have a list of what they are, what they are for, and who prescribed them (if they are not over the counter). When working in community mental health, Faith used to make copies of medication orders for her clients who consistently had police interactions and staple her business card to the list. This demonstrated that their medications were their own, prescribed and procured legally, and that the person in question had a case manager that could be contacted with further concerns.

CONCLUSION: NAVIGATING THE NEUROPHOBIC WORLD TOGETHER

When Elly and Joe began their relationship in 2009, it was similar to a medieval marriage. Through combining finances and working in the same industry, they were able to better streamline the labor and costs involved with living in capitalist society. But over the following years, their roles shifted to align with their core strengths. Joe was more adept at broader strategy and systems thinking, while Elly was fantastic at implementing these systems, communicating them to staff, and figuring out how they would actually work in practice. Within five years, they were surprised to realize that the union made each of them want to be their best selves for each other. Generally speaking, the difference between modern and historical romance is that nowadays, you aren't getting married for the extra farmhand. It is much more likely that you are seeking partnership to find someone who makes you want to become a better person.

But relationships take work, regardless of whether or not either partner is autistic. As we've discussed in this book, relationships require intent, cooperation, and effort from both parties, and sometimes a couples counselor too. The most important part of any relationship, interabled or not, is creating and agreeing on a set of mutually accepted and respected guidelines. These guidelines should make all parties happy, emotionally fulfilled, and able to grow as people—a sum that is greater than its individual parts. Guidelines are also key to maintaining trust; if you cannot trust each other, a relationship is impossible. When difficulties arise, try to deal with the little things before they become dire, and focus on rebuilding trust through understanding and empathy.

And although understanding and empathy are vital to any relationship, these things may require particular thought and care in interabled partnerships. As we've learned in the preceding chapters, much of this comes down to communication. It can be very beneficial to give feedback to your autistic partner on other people's perceptions and expectations of them. In turn, listen to your partner at length, take in their perspective, and understand how their interactions result in all kinds of social difficulties and discrimination in work, education, and other facets of life. Repeating that information back to them can help them to see that their lived experience is real.

Many autistics are desperately struggling to hold on by a thread in a hostile and bewildering world. Relationships are a powerful way to braid that thread into a rope strong enough to pull a person up out of the darkness. And maybe, together, all of those braided threads can then become the shiny new clothes that we can wear while we reflect on how far we've grown together and how great we feel now. Relationships save lives and help us move towards our meaning and purpose, regardless of our neurology. They help us to see things that are important to us that we couldn't figure out on our own. Relationships are never about bending people to our will or forcing them to do our bidding. Don't let your partner treat you like they are your child or your boss. Don't treat your partner like you are their parent. Relationships are a two-way street where we also learn to understand our own hang-ups and childhood trauma—and work through it all—together.

Now that you've finished reading this book, we hope you come away feeling seen, with some new perspectives and skills to help you strengthen your romantic partnership(s) and your relationships generally. It's easy for an allistic person to fall into bad habits of perceiving the autistic person in their life as deficient, strange, vexing, or controlling. We hope we've been able to help you see whatever relationship difficulties you may experience more clearly, and maybe even overcome some of them by shifting your mindset or negotiating new relationship rules. You and your partner can have—and deserve to have—a healthy, loving, supportive relationship based on trust and respect. Use the skills you've learned here to make it happen.

RECOMMENDED READING AND RESOURCES

For more information and perspective about autism, relationships, trauma, and other topics covered in this book, check out these resources:

Asperger's Children: The Origins of Autism in Nazi Vienna by Edith Sheffer—This unflinching history investigates Nazi psychiatrists during the bloody Third Reich, the persecution of people perceived not to have social skills, and attempts to force autistic people to fit fascist ideas of productivity or be killed en masse.

The Autism Relationships Handbook: How to Thrive in Friendships, Dating, and Love—This is the book Joe and Faith wrote for autistic people who are in relationships (or who want to be). If you are reading this book to focus on being a better partner, you can have your partner read the first book in our autism series so they can focus on their part.

The Autism FAQ: Everything You Wanted to Know About Diagnosis & Autistic Life—Another one of our books, this is an FAQ on autism that interprets and refutes much of the information out there, shares the most recent research, and explores perspectives on what this research might mean for future work. This will be helpful if you are new to neurodiversity or if you are explaining your partner's neurology to someone else who is new to autism.

The Body Keeps the Score: Brain, Mind, and Body in the Healing of Trauma by Bessel van der Kolk—An intense exploration of trauma, this book focuses particularly on the effects of chronic traumatic stress in childhood as opposed to the effects of singular traumatic events.

The Electricity of Every Living Thing: A Woman's Walk in the Wild to Find Her Way Home by Katherine May—This book is about the author's adulthood diagnosis of autism, which came after she recognized her struggles with motherhood. She picks through her childhood and adult behaviors, sharing them with the reader in a manner that shows how easy it is to dismiss the signs of neurodivergence.

The Five Love Languages: How to Express Heartfelt Commitment to Your Mate by Gary Chapman—If you can get past the heteronormative and religious trappings, this small book offers valuable insight and practical approaches to showing your partner love in the way that is most meaningful to them (and seeing how they may already be showing you love in ways you're not used to recognizing).

Good Trouble: Building a Successful Life and Business with Asperger's—This is Joe's account of growing up as an undiagnosed autistic and learning from mistakes made along the way.

How to Keep House While Drowning: A Gentle Approach to Cleaning and Organizing by KC Davis—This guide to household management, housework, and self-compassion is written by a therapist and is particularly aimed at helping neurodivergent people figure out how to maintain a functional home. Allistic readers can get some good housework tips as well as insight into their autistic partner's perspective and needs.

In a Different Key—This PBS documentary traces a lot of the social history and discrimination that autistic people face, documenting a hidden civil rights movement in the process.

Neurotribes: The Legacy of Autism and the Future of Neurodiversity by Steve Silberman—This book details the complicated social history of autism, explaining how this history was tied up with eugenics before the emergence of the modern pride movement.

Unfuck Your Brain: Using Science to Get Over Anxiety, Depression, Anger, Freak-outs, and Triggers—Faith's small, powerful book explains how anyone can recover from trauma.

Unfuck Your Boundaries: Build Better Relationships Through Consent, Communication, and Expressing Your Needs—Another of Faith's books, this is essential reading for anyone who wants to make sure they are treating themself and those around them with the utmost respect.

Unfuck Your Intimacy: Using Science for Better Relationships, Sex, and Dating—Faith wrote this to help all people figure out the relationships they want and the relationships they have. If you're looking for more about getting your sex life on track, this is a great resource.

FOR THOSE WHO ARE LOOKING FOR RELATABLE FICTION FEATURING ALLISTIC-AUTISTIC RELATIONSHIPS:

Autistic romance novelist Helen Hoang's first book, *The Kiss Quotient*, is a great depiction of a relationship between an autistic woman and an allistic man; in her second book, *The Bride Test*, the genders are switched.

Talia Hibbert is an autistic romance novelist who has written autistic characters into a number of her books—*A Girl Like Her* features an autistic woman and an allistic man, and *Act Your Age, Eve Brown* is about a relationship between two autistic characters.

You might also enjoy *The Rosie Project* and sequels by Graeme Simsion, who is neurotypical but also really seems to know what he's talking about. These books are funny.

IF YOU LISTEN TO PODCASTS, CHECK THESE OUT:

Aftereffect is the story of an autistic man who is completely, thoroughly failed by the system.

Autism's First Child documents the life of the first person diagnosed with autism, Donald Gray Triplett, who was born in 1933.

The Loudest Girl in the World is radio reporter Lauren Ober's candid and at times very funny story of being diagnosed in her 40s and seeking out other autistic women to be friends with.

The *Invisibilia* episode "Frame of Reference" from July 8, 2016, is a great window into what it's like to be autistic.

The *Hidden Brain* episode "How to Complain Productively" from December 19, 2022, isn't exclusively about autism, but it touches extensively on how our brains crave validation of a perceived injustice we've experienced when, in fact, a reframing of our problem is so much more helpful to moving forward with our lives. Autistic partners are so quick to find pragmatic solutions to complaints that this research may help you find even more value in your partner.

REFERENCES

Alvares, G. A., Bebbington, K., Cleary, D., Evans, K., Glasson, E. J., Maybery, M. T., Pillar, S., Uljarević, M., Varcin, K., Wray, J., & Whitehouse, A. J. O. (2019). The misnomer of "high functioning autism": Intelligence is an imprecise predictor of functional abilities at diagnosis. *Autism, 24*(1), 221–232. https://doi.org/10.1177/1362361319852831

American Psychiatric Association. (2022). Diagnostic and statistical manual of mental disorders (5th ed., text revision). American Psychiatric Association Publishing.

Attanasio, M., Masedu, F., Quattrini, F., Pino, M. C., Vagnetti, R., Valenti, M., & Mazza, M. (2021). Are autism spectrum disorder and asexuality connected? *Archives of Sexual Behavior, 51*(4), 2091–2115. https://doi.org/10.1007/s10508-021-02177-4

Baribeau, D. A., Dupuis, A., Paton, T. A., Scherer, S. W., Schachar, R. J., Arnold, P. D., Szatmari, P., Nicolson, R., Georgiades, S., Crosbie, J., Brian, J., Iaboni, A., Lerch, J., & Anagnostou, E. (2017). Oxytocin receptor polymorphisms are differentially associated with social abilities across neurodevelopmental disorders. *Scientific Reports, 7*(1). doi.org/10.1038/s41598-017-10821-0

Bolognani, F., Del Valle Rubido, M., Squassante, L., Wandel, C., Derks, M., Murtagh, L., Sevigny, J., Khwaja, O., Umbricht, D., & Fontoura, P. (2019). A phase 2 clinical trial of a vasopressin V1a receptor antagonist shows improved adaptive behaviors in men with autism spectrum disorder. *Science Translational Medicine, 11*(491). doi.org/10.1126/scitranslmed.aat7838

Bourzac, K. (2012, November 29). *Long-term studies chart autism's different trajectories.* Spectrum. Retrieved January 2, 2023. https://spectrumnews.org/news/long-term-studies-chart-autisms-different-trajectories/

Bush, H. H., Williams, L. W., & Mendes, E. (2020). Brief report: Asexuality and young women on the autism spectrum. *Journal of Autism and Developmental Disorders, 51*(2), 725–733. https://doi.org/10.1007/s10803-020-04565-6

Carr, M. E., Moore, D. W. & Anderson, A. (2014). Goal setting interventions: Implications for participants on the autism spectrum. *Review Journal of Autism and Developmental Disorders, 1,* 225–241. doi.org/10.1007/s40489-014-0022-9

Case Western Reserve University. (n.d.). *Study shows autistic brains create more information at rest.* EurekAlert! Retrieved December 14, 2022, from eurekalert.org/news-releases/710474

Cassidy, S., Bradley, L., Shaw, R., & Baron-Cohen, S. (2018). Suicidality and non-suicidal self-injury in adults with autism spectrum conditions. Paper presented at the International Society for Autism Research 2018 Annual Conference, Rotterdam, Netherlands.

Cassidy, S. A., Gould, K., Townsend, E., Pelton, M., Robertson, A. E., & Rodgers, J. (2020). Is camouflaging autistic traits associated with suicidal thoughts and behaviours? Expanding the interpersonal psychological theory of suicide in an undergraduate student sample. *Journal of Autism and Developmental Disorders, 50*(10), 3638–3648. doi.org/10.1007/s10803-019-04323-3

Cazalis, F., Reyes, E., Leduc, S., & Gourion, D. (2022). Evidence that nine autistic women out of ten have been victims of sexual violence. *Frontiers in Behavioral Neuroscience, 26.* doi.org/10.3389/fnbeh.2022.852203

CDC estimate on autism prevalence increases by nearly 10 percent, to 1 in 54 children in the U.S. (n.d.). Autism Speaks. Retrieved January 7, 2023, from https://www.autismspeaks.org/press-release/cdc-estimate-autism-prevalence-increases-nearly-10-percent-1-54-children-us

Centers for Disease Control and Prevention. (2022, March 31). *What is autism spectrum disorder?* Centers for Disease Control and Prevention. Retrieved June 9, 2022, from cdc.gov/ncbddd/autism/facts.html

Chan, M. M., & Han, Y. M. (2020). Differential mirror neuron system (MNS) activation during action observation with and without social-emotional components in autism: A meta-analysis of neuroimaging studies. *Molecular Autism, 11*(1). doi.org/10.1186/s13229-020-00374-x

Chen, A. (2016). *For centuries, a small town has embraced strangers with mental illness*. NPR. Retrieved January 4, 2023, from https://www.npr.org/sections/health-shots/2016/07/01/484083305/for-centuries-a-small-town-has-embraced-strangers-with-mental-illness

Chen, M. H., Pan, T. L., Lan, W. H., Hsu, J. W., Huang, K. L., Su, T. P., Li, C. T., Lin, W. C., Wei, H. T., Chen, T. J., & Bai, Y. M. (2017). Risk of suicide attempts among adolescents and young adults with autism spectrum disorder: A nationwide longitudinal follow-up study. *Journal of Clinical Psychiatry, 78*(9), e1174–e1179. doi.org/10.4088/JCP.16m11100

Crespi, B. J. (2016). Autism as a disorder of high intelligence. *Frontiers in Neuroscience, 10*, 300. doi.org/10.3389/fnins.2016.00300

Culpin, I., Mars, B., Pearson, R. M., Golding, J., Heron, J., Bubak, I., Carpenter, P., Magnusson, C., Gunnell, D., & Rai, D. (2018). Autistic traits and suicidal thoughts, plans, and self-harm in late adolescence: Population-based cohort study. *Journal of the American Academy of Child and Adolescent Psychiatry, 57*(5), 313–320. doi.org/10.1016/j.jaac.2018.01.023

Dattaro, L. (2020). *Largest study to date confirms overlap between autism and gender diversity*. Spectrum. doi.org/10.53053/wnhc6713

Diamond, A. (2022, October 29). *How to sharpen executive functions: Activities to hone brain skills*. ADDitude. Retrieved December 2, 2022, from additudemag.com/how-to-improve-executive-function-adhd/

Ekern, B. (2016, March 31). *Understanding the difference between a feeding and eating disorder in your child*. Eating Disorder Hope. Retrieved December 2, 2022, from eatingdisorderhope.com/blog/understanding-the-difference-between-a-feeding-and-eating-disorder-in-your child

Fast-growing independent publishers, 2022. (2022, April 22). Publishers Weekly. Retrieved December 14, 2022, from publishersweekly.com/pw/by-topic/industry-news/publisher-news/article/89118-fast-growing-independent-publishers-2022.html

Fox, M. (2020, May 11). *First US study of autism in adults estimates 2.2% have autism spectrum disorder*. CNN. Retrieved July 13, 2022, from cnn.com/2020/05/11/health/autism-adults-cdc-health/index.html

Gallitto, E., & Leth-Steensen, C. (2015). Autistic traits and adult attachment styles. *Personality and Individual Differences, 79*, 63–67. doi.org/10.1016/j.paid.2015.01.032

George, R., & Stokes, M. A. (2018). Sexual orientation in autism spectrum disorder. *Autism Research: Official Journal of the International Society for Autism Research, 11*(1), 133–141. doi.org/10.1002/aur.1892

Gibbs, V., Hudson, J., & Pellicano, E. (2022). The extent and nature of autistic people's violence experiences during adulthood: A cross-sectional study of victimisation. *Journal of Autism and Developmental Disorders*. doi.org/10.1007/s10803-022-05647-3

Gravitz, L. (2018, September 26). *At the intersection of autism and trauma*. Spectrum. Retrieved from https://www.spectrumnews.org/features/deep-dive/intersection-autism-trauma/

Hall-Lande, J., Hewitt, A., Mishra, S., Piescher, K., & LaLiberte, T. (2014). Involvement of children with autism spectrum disorder (ASD) in the child protection system. *Focus on Autism and Other Developmental Disabilities, 30*(4), 237–248. doi.org/10.1177/1088357614539834

Head, T. (2021, August 9). *100 years of forced sterilizations in the U.S.* ThoughtCo. Retrieved July 20, 2022, from thoughtco.com/forced-sterilization-in-united-states-721308

Hedley, D., Uljarević, M., Foley, K. R., Richdale, A., & Trollor, J. (2018). Risk and protective factors underlying depression and suicidal ideation in autism spectrum disorder. *Depression and Anxiety, 35*(7), 648–657. doi.org/10.1002/da.22759

Hirvikoski, T., Boman, M., Chen, Q., D'Onofrio, B., Mittendorfer-Rutz, E., Lichtenstein, P., Bölte, S., & Larsson, H. (2018). Suicidality and familial liability for suicide in autism: A population based study. Paper presented at the International Society for Autism Research 2018 Annual Conference, Rotterdam, Netherlands.

Hirvikoski, T., Mittendorfer-Rutz, E., Boman, M., Larsson, H., Lichtenstein, P., & Bölte, S. (2016). Premature mortality in autism spectrum disorder. *British Journal of Psychiatry, 208*(3), 232–238. doi.org/10.1192/bjp.bp.114.160192

Im, D. S. (2016). Trauma as a contributor to violence in autism spectrum disorder. *Journal of the American Academy of Psychiatry and the Law, 44*(2), 184–192.

Jack, C. (n.d.). *Can a person with autism fall in love?* Psychology Today. Retrieved January 7, 2023, from https://www.psychologytoday.com/us/blog/women-autism-spectrum-disorder/202110/can-person-autism-fall-in-love

Jenco, M. (2021, December 2). *Autism rate rises to 1 in 44, early identification improves.* AAP News. Retrieved July 13, 2022, from publications.aap.org/aapnews/news/18816/Autism-rate-rises-to-1-in-44-early-identification?searchresult=1%3Fautologincheck

Kirby, A. V., Bakian, A. V., Zhang, Y., Bilder, D. A., Keeshin, B. R., & Coon, H. (2019). A 20-year study of suicide death in a statewide autism population. *Autism Research: Official Journal of the International Society for Autism Research, 12*(4), 658–666. doi.org/10.1002/aur.2076

Kolves, K., Fitzgerald, C., Nordentoft, M., Wood, S. J., & Erlangsen, A. (2021). Assessment of suicidal behaviors among individuals with autism spectrum disorder in Denmark. *JAMA Network Open, 4*(1). doi.org/10.1001/jamanetworkopen.2020.33565

Landén, M., & Rasmussen, P. (1997). Gender identity disorder in a girl with autism—a case report. *European Child & Adolescent Psychiatry 6*, 170–173. doi.org/10.1007/BF00538990

Lisitsa, E. (2022, July 10). *The four horsemen: The antidotes.* Gottman Institute. Retrieved December 22, 2022, from https://www.gottman.com/blog/the-four-horsemen-the-antidotes/

Lobregt-van Buuren, E., Hoekert, M., & Sizoo, B. (2021). Autism, adverse events, and trauma. In A. M. Grabrucker (Ed.), *Autism Spectrum Disorders* [Internet]. Exon Publications. ncbi.nlm.nih.gov/books/NBK573608/ doi: 10.36255/exonpublications.autismspectrumdisorders.2021.trauma

Mayes, S. D., Gorman, A. A., Hillwig-Garcia, J., & Syed, E. (2013). Suicide ideation and attempts in children with autism. *Research in Autism Spectrum Disorders, 7*(1), 109–119. doi.org/10.1016/j.rasd.2012.07.009

McDonnell, C. G., Boan, A. D., Bradley, C. C., Seay, K. D., Charles, J. M., & Carpenter, L. A. (2019). Child maltreatment in autism spectrum disorder and intellectual disability: Results from a population-based sample. *Journal of Child Psychology and Psychiatry, and Allied Disciplines, 60*(5), 576–584. doi.org/10.1111/jcpp.12993

Mills, D. (2016, April 1). *Why people with autism die at a much younger age.* Healthline. Retrieved January 7, 2023, from https://www.healthline.com/health-news/why-people-with-autism-die-at-younger-age

Network, M. S. I. A. (2018, July 24). *The link between autism and suicide risk.* Interactive Autism Network. Retrieved June 15, 2022, from autismspectrumnews.org/the-link-between-autism-and-suicide-risk/

New shocking data highlights the autism employment gap. (n.d.). National Autistic Society. Retrieved December 9, 2022, from https://www.autism.org.uk/what-we-do/news/new-data-on-the-autism-employment-gap

O'Halloran, L., Coey, P., & Wilson, C. (2022). Suicidality in autistic youth: A systematic review and meta-analysis. *Clinical Psychology Review, 93.* doi.org/10.1016/j.cpr.2022.102144

Parker, K. J., Oztan, O., Libove, R. A., Mohsin, N., Karhson, D. S., Sumiyoshi, R. D., Summers, J. E., Hinman, K. E., Motonaga, K. S., Phillips, J. M., Carson, D. S., Fung, L. K., Garner, J. P., & Hardan, A. Y. (2019). A randomized placebo-controlled pilot trial shows that intranasal vasopressin improves social deficits in children with autism. *Science Translational Medicine, 11*(491). doi.org/10.1126/scitranslmed.aau7356

Pérez Velázquez, J. L., & Galán, R. F. (2013). Information gain in the brain's resting state: A new perspective on autism. *Frontiers in Neuroinformatics, 7.* doi.org/10.3389/fninf.2013.00037

Popa-Wyatt, M. (2020). Reclamation: Taking back control of words. *Grazer Philosophische Studien, 97*(1), 159–176. doi.org/10.1163/18756735-09701009

Researchers call for the term "high functioning autism" to be consigned to history. (n.d.). Telethon Kids Institute. Retrieved December 9, 2022, from telethonkids.org.au/news--events/news-and-events-nav/2019/june/researchers-call-for-term-high-functioning-autism/

Richa, S., Fahed, M., Khoury, E., & Mishara, B. (2014). Suicide in autism spectrum disorders. *Archives of Suicide Research: Official Journal of the International Academy for Suicide Research, 18*(4), 327–339. doi.org/10.1080/13811118.2013.824834

Rudy, L. J. (n.d.). *What is stimming?* Verywell Health. Retrieved September 8, 2022, from verywellhealth.com/what-is-stimming-in-autism-260034

Schultz, R., Chevallier, C., & Kohls, G. (2022, May 5). Social motivation, reward and the roots of autism. Spectrum. Retrieved January 7, 2023, from https://www.spectrumnews.org/opinion/viewpoint/social-motivation-reward-and-the-roots-of-autism/

Sex ed for self-advocates. (2022, November 2). Organization for Autism Research. Retrieved December 22, 2022, from https://researchautism.org/self-advocates/sex-ed-for-self-advocates/

Simone, R. (2010). *Asperger's on the job: Must-have advice for people with Asperger's or high functioning autism and their coworkers, educators, and advocates.* Future Horizons Incorporated.

Sinclair, J. (2012) Don't mourn for us. *Autonomy, the Critical Journal of Interdisciplinary Autism Studies, 1*(1). Retrieved August 30, 2022, from philosophy.ucsc.edu/SinclairDontMournForUs.pdf

Smith, A. (2009). Emotional empathy in autism spectrum conditions: Weak, intact or heightened? *Journal of Autism and Developmental Disorders, 39,* 1747–1748.

Song, Z., & Albers, H. E. (2018). Cross-talk among oxytocin and arginine-vasopressin receptors: Relevance for basic and clinical studies of the brain and periphery. *Frontiers in Neuroendocrinology, 51,* 14–24. doi.org/10.1016/j.yfrne.2017.10.004

Spence, J. (2020, February 18). *Nonverbal communication: How body language & nonverbal cues are key.* Lifesize. Retrieved January 7, 2023, from https://www.lifesize.com/blog/speaking-without-words/

Spencer, L., Lyketsos, C. G., Samstad, E., Dokey, A., Rostov, D., & Chisolm, M. S. (2011). A suicidal adult in crisis: An unexpected diagnosis of autism spectrum disorder. *American Journal of Psychiatry, 168*(9), 890–892. doi.org/10.1176/appi.ajp.2011.10091261

Stagg, S. D., & Belcher, H. (2019). Living with autism without knowing: Receiving a diagnosis in later life. *Health Psychology and Behavioral Medicine, 7*(1), 348–361, doi.org/10.1080/2164 2850.2019.1684920

Stamatakis, J. C. (2011, November 1). *Are we biologically inclined to couple for life?* Scientific American. Retrieved January 7, 2023, from https://www.scientificamerican.com/article/are-we-biologically-inclined/

Stavropoulos, K. K. M., Bolourian, Y., & Blacher, J. (2018). Differential diagnosis of autism spectrum disorder and post traumatic stress disorder: Two clinical cases. *Journal of Clinical Medicine, 7*(71), doi.org/10.3390/jcm7040071_

Strang, J. F., Janssen, A., Tishelman, A., Leibowitz, S. F., Kenworthy, L., McGuire, J. K., Edwards-Leeper, L., Mazefsky, C. A., Rofey, D., Bascom, J., Caplan, R., Gomez-Lobo, V., Berg, D., Zaks, Z., Wallace, G. L., Wimms, H., Pine-Twaddell, E., Shumer, D., Register-Brown, K., . . . Anthony, L. G. (2018). Revisiting the link: Evidence of the rates of autism in studies of gender diverse individuals. *Journal of the American Academy of Child and Adolescent Psychiatry, 57*(11), 885–887. doi.org/10.1016/j.jaac.2018.04.023

Szalavitz, M. (2016, March 1). *Autism—it's different in girls.* Scientific American. Retrieved January 7, 2023, from https://www.scientificamerican.com/article/autism-it-s-different-in-girls/

The hidden danger of suicide in autism. (2020, August 5). Spectrum. Retrieved June 15, 2022, from spectrumnews.org/features/deep-dive/hidden-danger-suicide-autism/

Turban, J. L., & van Schalkwyk, G. I. (2018). "Gender dysphoria" and autism spectrum disorder: Is the link real? *Journal of the American Academy of Child and Adolescent Psychiatry, 57*(1), 8–9. doi.org/10.1016/j.jaac.2017.08.017

U.S. Department of Health and Human Services. (n.d.). *Ask suicide-screening questions (ASQ) toolkit.* National Institute of Mental Health. Retrieved June 15, 2022, from nimh.nih.gov/research/research-conducted-at-nimh/asq-toolkit-materials

van Schalkwyk, G. I., Klingensmith, K., & Volkmar, F. R. (2015). Gender identity and autism spectrum disorders. *Yale Journal of Biology and Medicine, 88*(1), 81–83.

Vedantam, S. (Host). (2022, December 12). The secret to gift giving. [Audio Podcast Episode] In *Hidden Brain*. Hidden Brain Media. hiddenbrain.org/podcast/the-secret-to-gift-giving/

Walker-Miller, C. (2020, September 13). *Equity includes opportunity for Michiganders with disability.* Detroit Free Press. Retrieved December 9, 2022, from freep.com/story/opinion/contributors/2020/09/13/equity-disabled-michiganders-autism/3472068001/

Wang, W., Liu, J., Shi, S., Liu, T., Ma, L., Ma, X., Tian, J., Gong, Q., & Wang, M. (2018). Altered resting-state functional activity in patients with autism spectrum disorder: A quantitative meta-analysis. *Frontiers in Neurology, 9.* doi.org/10.3389/fneur.2018.00556

Warrier, V., Greenberg, D. M., Weir, E., Buckingham, C., Smith, P., Lai, M. C., Allison, C., & Baron-Cohen, S. (2020). Elevated rates of autism, other neurodevelopmental and psychiatric diagnoses, and autistic traits in transgender and gender-diverse individuals. *Nature Communications, 11*(1). doi.org/10.1038/s41467-020-17794-1

Wiggins, L. D., Durkin, M., Esler, A., Lee, L., Zahorodny, W., Rice, C., Yeargin-Allsopp, M., Dowling, N. F., Hall-Lande, J., Morrier, M. J., Christensen, D., Shenouda, J., & Baio, J. (2019). Disparities in documented diagnoses of autism spectrum disorder based on demographic, individual, and service factors. *Autism Research.* doi.org/10.1002/aur.2255

World Health Organization. (n.d.). *Autism.* World Health Organization. Retrieved July 13, 2022, from who.int/news-room/fact-sheets/detail/autism-spectrum-disorders

World Health Organization. (2019). ICD-11: International Statistical Classification of Diseases and Related Health Problems. World Health Organization.

Yates, L., & Hobson, H. (2020). Continuing to look in the mirror: A review of neuroscientific evidence for the broken mirror hypothesis, EP-M model and STORM model of autism spectrum conditions. Retrieved July 20, 2022, from journals.sagepub.com/doi/10.1177/1362361320936945

ABOUT THE AUTHORS

Joe Biel is a self-made autistic publisher and filmmaker who draws origins, inspiration, and methods from punk rock and has been featured in *Time Magazine, Publishers Weekly, PBS, NPR, Spectator (Japan), G33K (Korea), and Maximum Rocknroll*. Biel is the author of dozens of books and over a hundred zines. joebiel.net

Dr. Faith G. Harper, LPC-S, ACS, ACN is a bad-ass, funny lady with a PhD. She's a licensed professional counselor, board supervisor, and certified sexologist with a private practice and consulting business in San Antonio, TX. She has been an adjunct professor and a TEDx presenter, and proudly identifies as a woman of color and uppity intersectional feminist.

Elly Blue is a writer and bicycle activist living in Portland, Oregon. She has been featured on *Democracy Now!*, in the *Oregonian*, and on *Oregon Public Broadcasting*. In addition to a dozen books, her work has appeared in *The Guardian, Grist, Bicycling Magazine* online, *Bitch, BikePortland*, and many other publications.